The Marital Arts
Create Your Marriage

Larry Stallman

Relationship Arts Press
Albany, New York

The Marital Arts

© 2013 Lawrence S. Stallman, Ph.D.

ISBN – 13: 978-0615945361
ISBN – 10: 0615945368

Library of Congress Control Number: 2014900611

Publisher: Relationship Arts Press
        872 Myrtle Ave.
        Albany, NY 12208

Cover sculpture by Larry Stallman
Cover Photograph by Janet Joseph
Title page sculpture by Larry Stallman
Blog and website at: http://www.themaritalarts.com

Acknowledgements

A project like this or any other, begins, literally at con-ception. I didn't choose the parents I had, nor, therefore, my school for marriage. I was lucky. Minna and Irving Stallman shared their lives during a different age. Many of their challenges, expectations and values seem so different from the ones we currently face, and yet they were strikingly similar. Each generation of marital partners strives to live, to love, to grow, to gather the resources needed to provide for themselves and their family, to share community with their fellows. to remove impasses, to find joy. Min and Irv modeled love and respect, and demonstrated through their actions that everyone counts all the time. For this I am truly grateful.

I would like to acknowledge the accidents of my birth. I have lived through "interesting" times. There have been wars and social upheavals; there have been enormous transformations in technology and communications; there have been seismic shifts in gender relations and in the pace of social change. I have seen the world's population grow from 2.5 billion to 7.2 billion. Everything that has occurred in the past 67 years has influenced my outlook and helped to shape me even as I recognize that the manner by which this happened is a mystery. I must admit, too, that because of the ways that I have floated through an almost infinite field of social, cultural, bio-chemical, political, and artistic-expressive forces my acknowledgements are flawed and deficient. I'm a product of my times; a time when ideas are written, played, sung, danced, photographed, acted on stage, screen, tv and computer screen, hung on walls and transmitted through the vapors... I've been exposed to so much that it is hard for me to tweeze out the influences of my thinking. I apologize to all those individuals who I don't acknowledge by name. I am thankful to have been shaped by them all.

I have some very specific people that I would like to thank: Some of my friends were generous enough to have waded through, and contributed their ideas to a very early version of this book: Dennis Gaffney, Tommy Holecek, Sylvie Kantorovitz, Bob Pettie, David Pettie, Sugi Pickard, Kim Ploussard, and Laura Whelan. Thank you all.

Thank you to my good friend Dr. Barbara Kuerer-Gangi for her insights and contributions to my discussion of attachment theory.

Thank you to another good friend, Ed Atkeson, for his helpful guidance in solving some of the problems of design and formatting of this book's pages.

Kate Cohen edited my manuscript, and I am thankful for her sharp eyes, her well tuned ears, and her good sense. She was enormously helpful in transforming my pile of thoughts into a book.

I would like to thank the hundreds of clients who have worked with me over the last 35 years and who have taken the risks and demonstrated the courage required to gain insights, make difficult changes and grow their relationships. They continue to educate and inspire me every day.

Finally, I would like to thank my honey, and partner in the Marital Arts, Rachelle Smith-Stallman. For 27 years we've been *feeling* the love (the easy part), and aspiring to *act lovingly* all the time (much more difficult). The process of dancing through the impasses of a marriage with a gifted partner, and of stepping around, over, and under the incessant demands of our inner babies has been an enormously important part of my personal growth and education and has made an invaluable contribution to the ideas presented in this book.

Thanks, also, to you, my reader, for picking up this book.

Every Artist was once an amateur.
—*Ralph Waldo Emerson*

Table of Contents

To create one's own world in any of the arts takes courage.

— *Georgia O'Keefe*

Introduction

When searching for the hidden temple of marital happiness it is good to have a map.
–Chi Shing Chen

After the last of the cake has been devoured, and the photo album is safely put away, we turn towards each other, blink, and our married life begins. We rarely think again of the purpose of our marriage or of the efforts required to sustain it. It just sort of ... rolls along. From our wedding day forward we act intuitively and often unconsciously. We have the best of intentions, usually based on the belief that "love will conquer all," but things happen and we find ourselves confused by situations that we never anticipated. Why is she so angry? Why am I so hurt? Why is there such distance between us?" We use the tools we have inherited and the ones we have gathered along our way, and we do the best we can.

None of us has attended a school for marriage. If we were ever asked the question, "Why are you doing this?" we answered, "Because we love each other and we want to spend our lives together," which is a very good answer. But we can *feel* love for each other without making the kind of commitment that marriage requires. What is the commitment? What are we committing to? What does this commitment really mean for our life together?

Here are the answers that I explore in this book: We are committed to helping each other define, pursue and achieve the best life possible; we are committed to helping each other grow and actualize ourselves in every possible way; we are committed to becoming everything we can be, and to helping each other become everything we can be. We will help each other grow morally and spiritually, sexually, materially, and socially; we will help each other become the best parents, grandparents, friends, and citizens; we will support each other in pursuit of our passions; we will help each other master our demons. We will develop skills and engage in a process that strives always to be loving and respectful. When we fail we will express remorse and forgiveness and re-commit to the process. We will both count *all the time*. We will be partners, and our marriage will be Art. If we find that our life paths really do diverge, if we are no longer able to find a way to share our lives, we will go our own ways, while maintaining the commitment of love and respect, because *this* commitment is forever.

We have all observed marriages that fill us with awe and, perhaps, some envy. The partners seem to glide through life together like an Olympic ice skating pair; spinning in a counterbalanced pas-de-deux, jumping and landing in elegant synchrony, one leaning back with perfect trust as the other holds and supports. They balance friendship and passion, spontaneity and discipline, closeness and space. They appear to be artists in their married life. How do they do it? This book represents my effort to understand the Marital Art, and to identify the qualities of the Marital Artist.

The idea of "art" is ancient, rich, and varied; the range of its expression is infinite. In this book I would like to focus on an art form that I will call the Marital Art. The Marital Artist devotes much of his or her energy to creating a marriage that is personally fulfilling, emotionally rewarding, and spiritually transcendent for both partners. Like any other artist, the Marital Artist develops his or her craft, and focuses on elements of intention, creativity, imagination, and process. The Marital Arts represent a set of beliefs, attitudes, and commitments that can contribute significantly to an enhanced experience of marriage, and, consequently, of life. In this book the reader will not find formulas, or recipes, or the suggestion that there is a "right" way to do a marriage. On the contrary, readers should understand that marriage can be as unique as the individuals who join to create it. It is *their* creation, *their* work of art, and the more "art" they bring to the process, the more satisfying the result will be. But it's not a free-for-all and we'll explore some of the ground rules.

As a psychologist and family therapist for over thirty-five years, I've had the privilege of working with hundreds of couples who have found themselves seeking a new way because, for one reason or another, their old way wasn't working. I have also studied dramatic arts, music, sculpture, and martial arts and I believe that the processes of the arts can be applied to the processes of marriage.

The Marital Arts reflect a set of attitudes, values, intentions, and skills that contribute to the lifelong process of creation and re-creation that is a marriage. The Marital Artist is a person who dedicates him- or her self to the pursuit of a transcendent marriage, and who never takes the process for granted. Awareness of these attitudes, values, intentions, and skills becomes a profoundly important part of the daily experience of life for the Marital Artist, in the same way that awareness of sound and rhythm is elemental to the musician's work; awareness of form, color, and line is essential to the painter; awareness of volume, form, and texture is vital for the sculptor; and awareness of movement is indispensable to the dancer. And like the martial artist, the Marital Artist is committed to pursuit of a centered, transcendent self-discipline that shapes all of the decisions of his or her life.

About the Use of Maps

You may have had the experience of opening up an old map and finding that your destination is not represented, or you've downloaded a map and a set of directions from the internet that don't get you where you want to go. Maps can be useful but they can also be misleading. Those of you motivated to pursue the Marital Arts and a "transcendent" marriage, should be skeptical of maps even as you make an effort to collect a variety of them written by those of us who have had the opportunity to spend time with hundreds of marriages in which partners are struggling with the same issues that you face every day. Remember though, that, as the philosopher and scientist Alfred Korzybski recognized, "the map is not the terrain." There are many mapmakers and although our observations are informed by our experiences, beliefs, and values, our maps reflect "our" truths and not "the" truth. Also, our maps reflect our understanding of the challenges of marriage in the context of our specific time and place.

There is nothing more admirable than two people who see eye-to-eye, keeping house as man and wife, confounding their enemies, and delighting their friends.
–Homer

If you've picked up this book you must be interested in "seeing eye to eye," with someone you call your spouse (or significant other, or committed partner). You're either married, or you're thinking about it. Maybe you're madly in love, or all your friends are getting married, or your biological clock is ticking and you've been struck with the feeling that it's time. Maybe you've been married for a few years or many years and you have some questions. Maybe you've been married in spirit for a long time and lack only the certificate. Maybe you'd like to marry your beloved, but the laws of your state won't permit it because your partner is of the same gender that you are. Perhaps you're thinking of calling it quits on a marriage that feels broken; or you and your spouse are frustrated by careers, children, homes, cars, pets, friends, or hobbies that occupy large chunks of the time that you would like to spend with each other. Maybe you're struggling with serious financial woes, illness, or sexual complaints that work their way into every argument. You watch helplessly as the sex, romance, playfulness, and friendship leak from your lives like air from a punctured tire. There are so many impasses capable of disrupting the marital journey. You simply want to cruise down the road to happiness, but you're finding that the road has been littered with a jagged obstacle course of irritations, disappointments, and frustrations.

This book contains no cookbook solutions. Rather, its various chapters will offer you a way of thinking about your relationship as art, and this will provide a foundation for the invention of solutions to anything that pops up.

I'm not going to promise you that this book can ensure your everlasting marital bliss any more than a book about musical composition can guarantee the creation of a great symphony. My goal is to guide you to a sense of personal commitment to achieve a partnership (if that's your choice) rooted in self-knowledge, self-discipline, creativity, empathy, compassion, humility, and love. We all need to respect the enormous number of variables that contribute to the making of a transcendent marriage, no less than to any other work of art.

A good marriage is not a birthright; in reality, the odds are against you. The odds are against you especially if you think that your marriage is a "thing" that you acquire down at the church, synagogue, mosque or city hall. As an eighth degree *martial* arts instructor once said, "You want a black belt? Here, take it. It will help you keep your pants up. It means nothing beyond that, unless you have assimilated the principles, values, commitments, and skills of the evolving martial artist." Those who succeed in marriage view marriage not as a "thing," but as a "process," a process very much like the process of art. Since the creative process always reflects your level of personal growth and evolution, marital partners must continually support each other's commitment to personal growth. You are pursuing fulfillment in your marriage and those who achieve this represent a very exclusive club: a High Honor Roll of sorts. Good for you!

In the many years that I have worked with couples, I have been impressed with how desperately they express the desire to be happy in their relationships. I have been saddened by how often two good people, starting out with the best of intentions, wanting so much to share a life of happiness, seem unable to create a partnership capable of achieving that goal. They make efforts to please their partners, yet feel unappreciated. They ask for seemingly simple things like trustworthiness, affection, sex, romance, cooperation, conversation, give and take, and understanding, and yet they often feel betrayed, abandoned, lonely, horny, sad, angry, and misunderstood. How does this happen? Let us count the ways, and see if we can develop some strategies for getting into the exclusive society of the Marital Artists.

In the chapters that follow we will examine some of the obstacles to the creation of Marital Art, and develop some strategies for avoiding them. There are some general themes that will weave through the chapters of the book. I will talk about intention and personal responsibility. I will often remind you that it's easier to *get* what you want if you *know* what you want and not simply what you *don't* want. I will emphasize commitment to personal growth as a marital value, and argue that the only person we have any hope of changing is ourself; *we will never change our partners.* It will be their job to change themselves if and when they want to. I will remind you, too, that in a successful marriage, everybody counts. All the time! (This sounds so simple and obvious during times of peace and tranquility, however, as we will see, it is not so simple when we are stressed, or at war over some perceived impasse!) Also, you will do well to remember that you are *always* married. Even when you are behaving independently, which is important and valuable, you are still part of the larger entity. I will refer to the spiritual idea of "transcendence," by which I imply no relationship to any name-brand religious discipline, but rather, the intentions and the practices that can take us beyond our inherited reflexes, biases and fallout from the serendipitous accidents of our lives. As Viktor Frankl said in *Man's Search for Meaning,*

> *"...the individual personality... remains essentially unpredictable. The basis for any predictions would be represented by biological, psychological or sociological conditions. Yet one of the main features of human existence is the capacity to rise above such*

conditions and transcend them. In the same manner, man ultimately transcends himself; a human being is self-transcending being."

Achieving consistent states of transcendence is rare, as rare as achieving a black belt in the martial arts; or creating a great painting or a timeless piece of music. These transcendent achievements involve a complex mixture of luck, self-knowledge, self-discipline, wisdom, values, and perseverance; practice, patience, and more practice. Like the martial arts, the Marital Arts represent a practice based on seeking and growing and require the realization that we are all works in progress; that the "we" represented by a marriage is in constant development, and that humility, a deep understanding that we are all beginners, will serve us better than arrogance. In a marriage none of us has the answers until we create them together. It is my contention that the practice of seeking transcendence is invaluable in achieving happiness in marriage (or anyplace else, for that matter).

We all come to the practice of any art with varying degrees of talent, experience, and motivation. Readers of this book do not need to be geniuses like Mozart or Michelangelo in order to strive for the creation of Marital Art. I trust that *all of us,* regardless of our starting point, can embrace the processes of Marital Art and grow with practice.

I would also like to say a word about the terms "marriage" and "marital." Among the unmarried are those who choose to live together in committed relationships without the official sanctification of a religious ceremony, or any

17

civic, legal recognition of their marriage. These committed relationships share many of the same features as marriages, with one symbolic step missing, namely, the marriage ceremony. It is not clear how, or whether that marriage ceremony changes the quality of a committed relationship, although it is hard to imagine that the public sharing of the commitment does not in some way add weight to the commitment, overtly communicate a seriousness of intention, and implicitly, if not explicitly, solicit support for the relationship from the community. The symbolic step of marriage cuts out some of the wiggle room, and provides a buffer against impulsive abandonment of the project when the going gets tough. Also, it is possible that many of the practical challenges of marriage, for instance sex, money, in-laws and extended families, children and ownership of property, among others, are managed differently by those who are committed to each other with and without the ceremony. I don't really know of any research that parses all of this out, and so for now, for our purposes, I will not worry about the distinction especially since in many places people who would otherwise be married cannot be, because of laws that preclude them from legal marriage on the basis of their gender preferences. I will assume that my readers understand that when discussing the Marital Arts, I am talking about *seriously* committed relationships.

The "case studies" related in this book represent composites of stories that I have heard from patients and friends. Names and details have been changed to conceal identities.

I have taken the liberty of employing the sayings of my *completely made-up, fictional, not-real,* but, I would like to think, wise, 13th century Chinese sage, Chi Shing Chen, whose simple, yet profound insights illuminate some of the most perplexing issues confronting the Marital Artist. I have also quoted some other *real* wise men and women who seem to "get it." I hope that you enjoy your adventure in the Marital Arts.

The Marital Artist:

- focuses, practices, learns, and grows;

- employs personal creativity, taking inspiration from an unlimited variety of sources;

- understands that marriages are creative processes and always have the qualities of a work in progress;

- sees impasses as opportunities and challenges, to be confronted, together with the beloved, employing energy, imagination, and joy;

- takes responsibility for every action, and lives every day with her or his partner, in the marriage that they are creating;

- seeks awareness of, acceptance of, and mastery over the accidents of birth, the lifelong personal demons, and the other natural impediments to creative marital transcendence.

Marriage is not a ritual or an end. It is a long, intricate, intimate dance together, and nothing matters more than your own sense of balance and your choice of partner.
—Amy Bloom.

Chapter 1 Some Thoughts about Marriage...

We are two drops of water, entering the raging river from different streams. We find each other, and flow to the ocean together.
—Chi Shing Chen

In the time of Chi Shing Chen, some manifestation of the institution of marriage had already existed for generations. As a revered fictional wise man of his time, Chi Shing Chen believed that marriage was the most natural state of union between a man and a woman, and yet he had a deep appreciation of the difficulties and paradoxes inherent in managing this arrangement. Some individuals, he knew, could live a life without marriage. But they were in the minority, and they had to work quite hard to develop alternatives to the solutions that marriage provided for the problems of human existence. Among these were the challenges of economic stability, of loneliness, of sex, of bearing and rearing children, and of maintaining stable societies.

Today, our notions of the concept of "marriage" are in transition. We used to think that we knew what it was. The

Gods got us together, presented us with the ground rules, made sure the ceremony adequately established the covenant between the young couple and Them, insisted that everyone understood that this *was* for better or worse, and then sent the couple off on their life journey together. The steps were clear: we pretty much grew up enough to stand on our own two feet, and we got married! That was it. That's what everyone did. (Except for the weird ones, and the pitiful, and the hopeless...)

Within the memory of most Westerners over the age of 50, the expectation was that completing the marriage ceremony was rung one on the ladder of adult responsibility and privilege, and if you were lucky and watched your step, you could climb to great heights of health and wealth and wisdom. If you slipped a bit, there were often others there (your friends and family and the community at large) to help you regain your footing. If you slipped *badly*, and crashed to the bottom, well, everyone would agree that it was a pity, and, for a while, thoughtful hours would be passed (depending on your era in history) down at the river bank, or the grist mill, the general store, the quilting bee, or the water cooler, discussing whose fault it was and why the Gods or the fates or the couple's own foolishness had determined such a pitiful failure. In the end, you either made it or you didn't. You climbed or crawled around, over and under the obstacles or you didn't. And there were always obstacles. Everyone had their stories. ("You have no idea what it was like during the Great Depression." "After your father's accident, I didn't know how we were going to make it." "We had to live with my in-laws for the first two years.")

The idea that marriage would be an inevitable aspect of our lives used to be axiomatic and most civilizations have created some way of sanctioning the form of relationship that we think of as marriage. There have usually been restrictions based on age, race, socio-economic status, and sexual orientation, but for the majority, it was a right of passage and it was what you did. You grew up, you got married, you had kids, and then you grew old, strolling hand and hand into the sunset together.

Before the era of easy and acceptable divorce, marriages were considered a permanent state of being; 'till death do you part. And if you discovered, after the vows were taken, that there was a hot, sexy number living in the next town who set your heart atwitter? Well, too bad. The Gods had neglected to introduce you to each other until after the ceremony, so, tough luck. If your partner was a loser, a drunk, a philanderer, an abuser, sexually uninspired, or a rotten cook, that was tough luck as well. (Remember, "...for better or worse," and that great old standard, "You made your bed, now lie in it.") If you grew old and fat and wrinkled and toothless and bald and ugly, and you were still together, and you died and were laid to rest for eternity in adjoining cemetery plots under a single shady canopy, that was a good thing, because it meant that you had made it. On to the afterlife!

We happen to live in a very challenging time for marriage; a time unique in history, according to Stephanie Coontz in *Marriage: A History*. For most of human history there were many external reasons for staying together that had very little to do with emotional needs beyond survival and conformance to community standards. Among these, traditionally, have been economic reasons like consolidation of land and other properties, the extension of kinship supports, and, later on, the Church and other religious injunctions. Today, for most of us Westerners, all of these extrinsic factors tend to be secondary to more intrinsic personal motivations, such as, dare we say it, "love." But, as Coontz points out, "What happens when love goes?" And what is "love" anyway? Is it that intoxicating rush of passion, lust, and obsession that characterizes the early weeks of romance and infatuation and is easily reducible to the attraction chemistry identified by recent discoveries in neuroscience and biochemistry? Or is it something else?

Regardless of the time in history, the rite of passage that was marriage was accomplished, for the most part, in the context of an unquestioning faith in the collective wisdom of the culture as reflected in lore and myth, and in the teachings of parents and spiritual leaders. This wisdom was reflected in the cultural traditions and laws that were passed down to provide answers to questions that no one even thought to ask until modern times. Why are we doing this? What will we get out of it? What are the alternatives? What if it doesn't work out? For many, no doubt, there was comfort in the clarity of the expectations. For the others it was tough luck. If you demurred, the consequences could range from the perception of "pathetic" (old spinster) to "suspicious" (eccentric bachelor), to the vicious and grotesque responses of an offended community (stoning the sodomite). Marriage is just what everyone did or at least was expected to do. Respectable alternatives were few (nun? priest? monk?) and the non-respectable alternatives were unspeakable.

It is only quite recently that some of us Westerners have begun to see ourselves more humbly in the context of a much larger universe. We understand that we are just a hop and a skip, a rotated pelvis, some cranial volume and a tool or two from being chimps or orangutans. Primates all, and at some level we're still trying to solve the problems that our primate forebears had to solve: how to survive, how to pass our genetic material on to the next generation and make sure it survives, and how to communicate our survival tricks to our progeny. The various traditions of marriage are among those survival tricks, like figuring out that combining copper and tin makes bronze. Cultures isolated by geography, language, and xenophobia all had their own tricks and traditions and they were not particularly inclined to make changes when these had been demonstrated to work for them.

A technological and global age like ours, in which we get to see how others live, provides us with perspective and an opportunity to recognize that maybe *our* cultural solutions to the problems of living aren't the only ones, or the best ones. This can be confusing. What are the criteria by which we choose the traditions that will work for us? Do we automatically default to the ones we were born into? What if they don't work so well?

The usefulness of marital traditions can be determined by assessing how well they serve our need to survive; how well they contribute to the health and vigor of our other social institutions; and how well they enhance the well-being of the coupled individuals (and their offspring) who are confronting the challenges of living.

So that about sums it up, right? Marital traditions are tools, like the wheel, the hammer, or the iPhone, which have emerged over time to serve our survival. If we weren't fortunate enough to have been born into the best possible set of traditions, passed down to us by our parents and the culture surrounding them, then what do we do? Do we shop for the best traditions available in the global marketplace, and employ them in our marriage? Will this provide a survival advantage for ourselves and our tribe. Is that the bottom line?

Very few of us would be happy to accept that assessment. We'd like to think that we can get more from our marriages than a mere survival advantage, important as that may be. We'd like to think that our marriages serve some higher order human potential for self-definition, for self-actualization, and spiritual transcendence; a potential that distinguishes us from the other primates. We 21st-century Western humans can change the direction of our institutions at any time and re-make our relationships in our continuously evolving efforts to define ourselves. Sexual mores have relaxed; couples can sleep together without marrying, and women no longer need to rely financially on a spouse. These days we even have acceptable alternatives to heterosexual marriage. Same-sex couples can live together in relative peace and even marry in a growing number of places. We have much more freedom than ever before in defining our intimate relationships. We have the power to transcend the accidents of our birth, and become more. What a gift. What a challenge.

Our impulse to bond is such a primitive, complex, and essential force, that cultures throughout the world have deemed it necessary to provide oversight through ritual and rite. Where this occurs, individuals, for better or worse, inherit a whole set of rules, spoken, written, or unspoken, concerning the details of the roles and expectations of marriage. The implication is that to be a "good" person, and to have a successful marriage, you must work very hard to perform your roles and to meet expectations.

But in today's Western societies, expectations and social injunctions have loosened to such an extent that they barely exist. Now it has become the responsibility of each individual to clarify his or her own vision of the relationship s/he wants; to choose partners, to define the nature of the relationship, to choose to maintain or discard the relationship over time, and, most problematically, to create the rules.

In cultures like ours the commitments to partnership and marriage are stressed by the competing commitments to individuality and to the actualization of self. We want to be part of the partnership, but we also want to maintain our own individual identities and boundaries. Marriage without socially defined, shared, and supported roles is very anxiety provoking. We never quite know what to do; at every step in the process we have to make it up. But roles and rules make us anxious; they inhibit us and thwart our creativity, personal expression, and actualization of self. This is the paradoxical social context in which modern marital partners find themselves, and it presents this challenge to aspiring Marital Artists: how can we create and re-create our marriage, over and over again, so that it reflects the transforming shapes of our needs and aspirations throughout our life together?

Marital Artists strive to maintain the understanding that their marriage is an organic, transforming process, and always a work in progress.

I'm a terrible cook, but if I could cook, I would see that as art as well. It's how much creative energy you put into something.

—Tracy Emin

Chapter 2 …And Some Thoughts About Art

Have no fear of perfection, you'll never reach it.
–Salvadore Dali

A traveler in a small Chinese village asked where he could find an artist to create a traditional Chinese ink scroll painting. He was told to look for an old man, a master artist, who lived at the end of a long alley at the edge of the town. The traveler found the old man and told him what he wanted. The old man sat in front of a blank silk scroll, meditated for a few moments and began to make deft, graceful strokes. Twenty minutes later he was done. The traveler looked at the painting with awe and told the old artist that he was very moved by the painting. He asked what he owed and the artist quoted a very high price. The traveler was taken aback, and said, with some embarrassment, "You are a great artist. Of this there is no doubt. But how can you charge so much. The painting only took you twenty minutes to make."

The old artist replied, "No, my son. You are mistaken. To make that painting took me 78 years."

What is the relationship between art and marriage? We usually think about art as something to appreciate hanging on a wall, or resting on a pedestal. We read moving words of literature or poetry, or we enjoy a dance, musical, or theatrical performance. How can a marriage be art?

The manifestations of art have changed through the ages. From the first carvings on cave walls, or totems made from wood or stone, art has evolved to serve the needs of the people who create it. Art serves different purposes in different times. It represents the way we perceive ourselves as humans and it reflects our deepest longings and yearnings; it expresses our sense of wonder and represents our efforts to understand and appreciate our place in the universe; it expresses our individuality as well as our shared humanity; it helps us understand our personal and interpersonal struggles; it provides fun and the pure joy of creating whimsical or imaginary worlds. Art has been influenced by nature and our perception of our environments, by political changes and the aftermath of wars, social movements, and cross influences resulting from population migrations, religious beliefs, discoveries in science, economics and marketing. It is shaped by the contributions of strong, creative, persuasive personalities; it is constantly transforming as we define and redefine ourselves.

For the artist, art is a way of life. It represents a commitment to the development of craft and insight, an outlook that is open, eager to learn, and ready to find inspiration everywhere. And although there are many ways to think about art, it is usually characterized by qualities of intentionality, creativity, imagination, and process. Artwork can have the depth of a Bach fugue or the grace and simplicity of a preschooler's craft project; the whimsy of a poem by Shel Silverstein or the spiritual illumination of a painting by Leonardo Da Vinci; the soulful inspiration of an Oscar Peterson piano solo, the disturbing anxiety of a Bergman movie, or the spirit pumping rhythms of a Santana rock tune; but in all cases the creators approach their task intentionally. This means that the artists engage their medium with a desire to take simple elements like words, paint, clay, metal, tone, rhythm, movement, or found objects, and transform them into intentional expressions of themselves. The process necessarily involves creativity and imagination, because without these, paint is just paint, and clay is just clay. It is the artist's intention, creativity, and imagination that are transformative.

Once we accept our ability to employ our intentionality, creativity, and imagination, we can choose any medium in which to create art. Art had existed for thousands of years before the saxophone was invented. But as soon as it was, people began to explore its possibilities, and players like John Coltrane pushed its artistic limits. Artists have taken mundane, utilitarian objects like chairs and dishes and transformed them into art. Architects have transformed our humble shelters into art, designers have transformed our vehicles into art, and chefs have transformed our meals into art. Why, with the application of intention, creativity, and imagination, can't our marriages be art?

Intentionality helps the Marital Artist remain aware that a fulfilling marriage is not a mythical magic spell that you fall under, or a state of grace provided by the Gods. Marriage is a process and Marital Art is an approach to the process that is intentional and informed. Like any other artistic process, its quality reflects values, skills, luck, perspicacity, support, insight, creativity, and imagination. Marital Artists don't need to have the genius of a Louis Armstrong. They simply need to cherish the *commitment* and the *process* more than any specific *outcome*.

All art involves process. The great art academies of the 16th century in Europe had well defined, rigid notions of process and inculcated within their students very specific values that supported training in a body of knowledge and in accepted methods of creation. This route ensured the maintenance of well-defined aesthetic standards. In modern times the processes of art have become much more self-consciously open to experimentation and reinvention. There are even schools of art that have emerged purely around a fascination with process, with interest in the final "product" only to the extent that it reveals this process.

Process art was an artistic movement of the 1960's that emphasized the process of creation more than the final "work" of art. Artists like Jackson Pollock embarked on the "journey" with an inherent motivation, rationale, and intentionality that informed the process. Art viewed this way leads to unforeseen outcomes, surprises that stimulate and "grow" the artist. There are no mistakes, but rather serendipitous opportunities to learn new techniques and strategies that get folded into the process and become available for intentional use the next time around.

[People] who feel free to make mistakes and to explore will also feel free to invent, create and find new ways to do things.
–Mary Ann Kohl

The kind of marital process that we will discuss in a later chapter shares an affinity with this view of process art.

Serious artists maintain a respectful relationship with their own emotional responses to their art. Their "truth" involves a personal honesty and a deep commitment to the work of revisiting their art until they realize their vision. They often don't get it "right" the first time around. That is, they often don't realize their ideal, with their first, or even subsequent, efforts. Sometimes they never get there, and that is acceptable to them because their life is dedicated to the effort, or process, more than to the product. For these artists one effort leads to another as they become inspired by serendipitous effects, accidental discoveries, and even "mistakes" that inspire new creative opportunities.

Serious artists also invest in the development of their craft, that is, the skills required to pursue the ideal embodiment of their artistic vision. They practice to achieve control over their line, or their tone or their movement so that they can use their skills to more closely approximate the inspired vision that they hold in their hearts and minds. Martial artists repeat the same forms, or *kata,* over and over again, as they try to approach perfection, all the time understanding that they will never get there.

Martial arts share other similarities with the *Marital* Arts (with the worst examples of each often appearing indistinguishable). At their most evolved, both strive to mature into manifestations of centeredness, grace, and power through a commitment to a process and a practice of self-discipline. The attitude underlying these commitments is less about work as drudgery, and more about work as an exciting process of creation and the quest for perfection.

Artists must confront the fear that the product or outcome will not be what they hope it will be. This fear is often at the root of artist's "block." We cannot simply let the process unfold if we are fearful, full of judgments or self-doubt. As an artist, it is important to accept the possibility that outcomes will surprise us or challenge us further. It is rare to ever have to concede that any outcome is a failure. There is an apocryphal story about Thomas Edison, not generally considered an artist (although he could be seen as a scientist with an artist's attitude) who supposedly tried hundreds of materials before he found the proper one for the filament of his first functional light bulb. When asked how he tolerated so much failure he said, "I have not failed. I've just found 1,000 ways that don't work." This attitude can go a long way in the process of any art. If Edison had been intimidated by failure, he may never have had the fortitude to keep going once he encountered his first series of impasses. Every outcome is just another beginning. If we are committed to the process we can challenge ourselves to overcome the fear of less-than-optimal outcomes and use the knowledge that we gain from our struggles to move the process forward. The lesson modeled by Edison is as important in art, and more specifically, Marital Art, as it is in science.

A loving heart is the beginning of all knowledge.
—*Thomas Carlyle*

Chapter 3 Magical Meetings

The awesome lightning bolt takes our breath away. But we must not forget that in the dark, a humble candle permits us to gaze into the eyes of our beloved.
–Chi Shing Chen

Love at first sight is easy to understand; it's when two people have been looking at each other for a lifetime that it becomes a miracle.
–Amy Bloom

She noticed him at the other end of the bar. His dark, wavy, hair was just visible under a cowboy hat. He had high cheekbones and dark piercing eyes. He wore a large silver belt buckle. She melted when he winked at her and flashed his dazzling smile. She thought, "Uh oh, here we go again." She knew that she had met this same man, or someone just like him many times before.

Their romance started out at 200 miles per hour (as they always did). It fizzled 3 months later when she discovered that his wink and smile routine was not reserved for her alone. He was a "loverboy," a "Don Juan," a "Lothario," a "heartbreaker."

If we were able to go back with a time machine and a slo-mo scanning camera, we could see that in another part of the bar, out with his friends, was a shorter man, an architect with thinning hair, who was nursing a beer and laughing as he stared at our heroine admiringly. She never noticed him, so blinded was she by her cowboy. Oh, well. Had she met the architect, she might have discovered that he was warm, very successful, and funny, that he kept himself in great shape, and that he had decided, after years of fooling around, that he was seriously ready for a committed relationship.

Unless something changes, Miss "left-in-the-dust-again-and-again" will never meet a man who is good long-term relationship material because those men are just "not her type." She laments to her friends, "Aren't there any good men out there?"

The Type

Our "type" connects with something primitive inside our being and makes our lights flicker and then explode. The incredible chemical fireworks that begin on sight are not rational and are usually not controllable. And the quest to recreate that "rush" can become literally addictive. However, that "crazy love" is not necessarily a very good prognosticator for "happily ever after," although we all know it can provide a very exciting ride. So, for our young lady with Silver Buckle Man, it's not likely that a good long-term relationship prospect will ever get through her filter, at least until she modifies her filter. And why would she do that? Meeting our "type" is fun and exciting, and, we think, full of promise. We feel things that take our breath away. Such meetings are often seen as mystical manifestations of fate or timing or luck.

Our "type" is a person who has the right mixture of superficial features that combine cues wired in by our early childhood experiences in our families of origin, along with a host of barely understood cultural influences, perhaps a few shakes of biochemical voodoo, and enough ambiguity to permit us to project our fantasies onto him or her. We often respond to the same "type" characteristics over and over again because we keep trying to complete some unfinished, unconscious psychological business. Our own personality "issues" strive for resolution by means of a quest for our "soulmate," or our complimentary opposite. For example, our "shyness" seeks a partner who is either "outgoing" or similarly "shy"; our ambition seeks a co-conspirator, or someone to rein us in and ground us; our narcissism seeks someone who enhances our self-image or validates our low self-esteem; our passivity seeks a determined proactive person or someone equally passive to validate our inaction. We see the parent of our children, or the hot showpiece who will evoke envy at office parties; we see a partner for our business, or our supportive "good parent" to soothe us in times of sorrow; we see someone of whom our parents will approve, or someone who we can use to stick it to our parents; we see a ticket to financial security, an answer to sexual frustrations, a spiritual soul mate, a playmate, a person with the social skills we lack, a person with the warm and supportive family we never had, someone who will keep us secure and safe, someone who will need us, someone fun, someone who will not make demands... The person we meet gives us just enough clues to support our fantasy, more or less. Our unconscious needs and desires fill in the blanks.

This reflexive emotional response to a "type" is usually beyond our control. It is part of the legacy of growing up to be the people we are; a distillation of the accidents of our birth. We are not stuck with it however. If you are not married yet, it is important to know whether your "type" possesses the qualities that will support your quest for Marital Art (if that's what you're looking for). If your "hypnotism by type" has led you into marriage with the wrong person and you feel stuck there at this time, you have work to do. If you are serious about creating Marital Art, and the person you once found to be your "type" has turned out to be a "partner in dysfunction," you need help in getting yourselves (or at least *yourself,* if your partner will not participate) into a relationship environment that will nurture you. Marital counseling can help you and your partner explore alternatives that may work better than the one you have. The recognition that the old, less-than-functional, attractions aren't working any more can be the impetus to change for both partners. Or it might reflect a need for some difficult decisions.

Unconscious Needs

Our needs can profoundly affect the processes of our relationships. As we just saw, our needs, especially unconscious needs, can contribute to our *choice* of partner by loading us with potentials that are triggered when we meet someone who satisfies our "type" requirements. Where do these unconscious needs and desires come from? The "unconscious needs and desires" are clouds formed in the primeval chaos of our beginnings and represent echoes of the unlabeled processes of our early lives. Often these processes establish themselves even before we have language to help us mentally describe and record our experiences. We encounter environments, people, interaction styles, repeating patterns of need gratification, traumatic events, nurturance styles, availability of resources, all before we have any means of categorizing them, labeling them, or becoming conscious of them. But they are deeply a part of us. If every time I was cold, my sensitive, empathic caretaker covered me and comforted me, my unconscious expectations of the world are going to be different than if my caretaker regularly neglected my comfort. The same can be said of my other needs such as nourishment, love and affection, trust, safety and security, material well-being, health care, and emotional support. If our needs aren't met in some fundamental way, we don't get away for free. The vacuum left unfilled haunts us as an *issue*

43

through our childhood, adolescent, and adult relationships, frequently without our conscious awareness. Often we expect others to complete this unfinished business for us. It can be part of the attraction that we find in the potential partners we meet.

Lois' father disappeared before she was 2 years old, and her mother was depressed and moody. It was difficult for Lois to get her needs for nurturance and positive parental attention met. Lois became quite skilled at reading her mother's moods and anticipating her needs. She found that she could get some compromised level of attention and regard from her mother by being "mommy's little helper." She got a reputation, quite early in life, of being a "very good, sweet girl," the "care-taking" skills she developed, made it easy for her to make friends with kids who were marginally accepted among all of the other kids, the "outcasts" and "losers". She knew, quite intuitively, how to make them feel safe and secure. They needed her, so they weren't going to abandon her and thus, she could feel emotionally safe. When it came time to pick romantic partners, she generally chose men who were less educated and less accomplished than she was, and who had interpersonal issues of one sort or another. Often they were "bad boys" who provided some excitement and drama for a while. She discovered that these "tough" but "fragile" men would always come back to her

*when their lives were in crisis, and she would al-
ways be there for them – until she wasn't. The sense
of emotional job security she felt, would eventually
give way to frustration and rage over what she
wasn't getting from the relationship, and she would
"dump the bastard." Then she would go on to find
another one.*

*Until it was pointed out in therapy, Lois had no in-
sight into the unconscious role that her early emotional skill-set development had on her later choices.*

Unconscious needs can create patterns of emotional behavior in our lives that get repeated in relationship after relationship. They bend and shape us in a particular way, like a
young ballerina whose training impels her to stand on a
movie ticket line in the second position. We learn strategies
for surviving in the context of our primary environments and
carry these forward. When functional they provide us with
useful skills and tools that help us make good choices and
fulfill our needs. When dysfunctional, they keep us running
into impassible obstacles and repetitive frustrations, and we
find ourselves either chronically dissatisfied or hopping from
one relationship to another.

But every marriage inevitably begins with a meeting.
Whether it's arranged by parents, or set up by friends,
whether you meet at a bar, or in college, or in the Army;
whether you met in third grade or on the job or in the Peace
Corps; in "the 'hood," or at "the Club," whether you were in-
troduced by your cousin Yolanda or the "yenta," you had to

meet somewhere. And when you met, something happened. A snowball started rolling down a hill. Our reactions during that first meeting depend as much, or more upon who *we* are than upon who the other person is. We are looking consciously and unconsciously for "something," and if this person doesn't show some promise of providing that "something," then we are not interested. If that person doesn't make it through our filtering system, that first meeting will probably be our last, unless the contact is a regular part of our lives (such as at work or school or in the neighborhood) or unless one person is skillful and persistent. Our perceptions, and thus our filters, are based on our histories, our hopes, and our fears, and, more immediately, the way these histories, hopes, and fears are manifested in our fantasies.

In a culture that, notwithstanding certain small ethnic subcultures, has eschewed arranged marriages, we can meet potential partners in infinite ways. But it is remarkable how many people we encounter who *don't* turn into romantic possibilities. Most of the thousands of people we pass in the supermarket, on trains, in classrooms, coffeehouses, houses of worship, and in all our other comings and goings do not trigger our romantic interest, or we don't trigger theirs. Our "filters" do the work of eliminating prospects without any conscious effort. However, some meetings do spark romantic interest, or, at least, grow on us, and blossom into love and long-term commitments or marriage. How could we predict that the friend of a friend, dragged to a party for a co-worker, while he was in town for two days visiting his sick cousin would turn out to be the man of Sandra's dreams? Why did Fred post his profile on the dating site on the same day that Carol decided that she was finally ready to go the internet-dating route? Why was Alex in Maria's third-grade class in the Bronx instead of in a third-grade class in Puerto Rico where he was born? Sometimes it's just a matter of two pairs of eyes meeting across a crowded room.

Now That We've Met...

Some of us are really good at meeting people. Others, are not so good. For those contemplating marriage or the transition to Marital Art, it is useful to understand that the skills that help us meet people are not necessarily the skills that help us develop and maintain successful, fulfilling long-term relationships. Our Silver Buckle Man above had a flair for meeting women. He was practiced and smooth. Women responded to his relaxed warmth and confidence. The problem is that he loved the game and had very little interest in the relationship. We can call that immaturity or addictive behavior, but it doesn't really matter from the standpoint of someone really looking for a partner. As a long term relationship partner he is definitely not going to make the grade.

Let's assume that the potential partners have met and there is some chemistry. Once we start to desire this other person, things begin to happen. We become infatuated, our biochemistry changes, we fall in love. We go nuts. We walk on clouds. We become unrecognizable to our friends. They laugh at us; we don't even notice; we are obsessed with our beloved. We want our beloved to love us too, and so we do everything we can to encourage his or her love. We look for signals that reveal what he or she wants from us, and we begin the process of trying to meet those expectations. It isn't even an effort. It feels very natural. While sharing this magical time together we make every effort not to disappoint, or to disappoint just enough to enhance desire. We conceal our dark sides; we show generosity and keep selfishness in check; we demonstrate concern and not indifference; we exhibit kindness and suppress pettiness and meanness; we are focused and not distracted; we are patient, not impatient; loving and flexible, not angry and controlling. We seem to have no needs, but care only about our beloved. The friction emanating from this kind of mutual narcissistic massage can create a great deal of heat. And, amazingly, it's not an "act" or a manipulation. This is exactly what we want to do. We've been transformed by the "spell" of love.

We can speculate that in the early stages of human evolution, the heat generated by this kind of high-friction bonding helped to get the baby-making process started and ensured the procreation of the species. As a long-term solution to the modern human problem of emotional and social adaptation, however, it may be lacking. Current divorce statistics suggest that, at least in most Western countries, it is a struggle to sustain committed relationships even long enough to raise the children. The chemical fire created in the early stages of a relationship doesn't seem capable of maintaining its heat long enough to provide a lifetime of happiness.

When I speak to couples years later and they list the litany of their complaints about each other, they almost always add that, "s/he wasn't like that when we met. S/he was wonderful in every way." Of course the "good" parts of our personalities, the "selfless" parts, are still observable years later, but at some point, when "the honeymoon is over," the rest of our personalities start to emerge. We can't suspend our needs indefinitely.

The reason is that this stage of infatuation, which is manifested in mutual self-less-ness or rigid self-masking roles, cannot be sustained. After months of "self-less" giving, our wants and ambivalences begin to reassert themselves. The biochemistry of attraction must be transfigured into a biochemistry of functional attachment or bonding; otherwise frustration and disappointment are inevitable. What used to be, "Anything you want, my darling," becomes something else.

"Honey, would you get me a cold glass of water?"
"Oh, sweetheart, I'm so tired, do you mind getting it yourself?"

"Precious one, would you rub my feet?"
"C'mon, will you? I'm exhausted too. Rub your own damn feet;"

"Would you quit your wonderfully fulfilling and financially rewarding career and move to Alaska with me so that I can fish for salmon?"

"That's it. You're an insane, selfish ^%$^& and I'm out of here."

Often we're not really looking for a long-term partner, and that's fine. Enjoy yourself. Sometimes we're not looking for "long-term" but "long-term" happens. A relationship that started out as a fling or a whim or "just one of those things" turns into something more. Some people continue to be okay with just taking it day by day and do this for a long, long time, sometimes forever. That's okay, too. But some of us want to go through life as part of a committed relationship and when that desire is realized things change. How do we make the decision to move from love, passion, fun, and relationship momentum, to the thought that "this person would make a good partner for me in my journey through life?"

By now we can see that the nature and chemistry of falling in love is not sufficient to ensure the functionality of long-term relationships, although it exerts a powerful force in getting us in, in stimulating sexual arousal, and in creating the bonds that keep us together during the early years. It is easy to speculate that the fear of this primal sexual tidal pull explains some of the many structures established over time by old cultures and religious traditions to diminish the risks of lust couplings. Wise observers, over time, have probably noticed that we sometimes get the "hots" for someone who is unlikely to do a good job of "happily ever after." That's why some of these cultures have demanded strict chaperoning of young people, asexual dress codes, perpetual separation of the genders, or have instituted parentally arranged marriages and have built in obstacles to abandoning a marriage impulsively or easily or ever.

Before we discuss the nature of functional long-term relationships and Marital Art, we should take a look at some of the ways that less functional long-term relationships happen. Mating efforts usually represent a compromise between the current state of our psychological adaptation no matter how dysfunctional, and the desire to enter the state of "relationship," no matter how unfulfilling or destined to fail. Among the dysfunctional opening gambits are those that represent an asymmetrical, but balanced, unspoken psychological agreement that exists from the earliest moments of the relationship. Examples of these are the relationships that operate on the level of the unspoken transactional games described by Eric Berne in his books such as *Transactional Analysis in Psychotherapy* and *Games People Play*. We could give these transactional games labels such as: *You Count and I Don't (or I Count and You Don't); I'm the Expert and You're the Dummy; or, You're Hurting and I've Come to Rescue You; or, We're Both so Hopeless that We Belong Together; or, I Have All the Needs and You Have None; or, You Know, and I Know, That I Have No Intention of Staying With You, but Let's See If You Can Get Me to Change My Mind.* We could describe many others.

When we are unaware of our own psychological needs, which usually date back to childhood, we are often destined to keep playing out these games over and over again. The players often do manage to get together at least for a while, sometimes a long while. All that is required is that each person accepts the rules of the game and the resulting compromised need gratification that results. Often the relationships begin to founder when one partner outgrows the game even if the other one continues to want to play.

Cathy was 16 when she met Ron, who was 26 at the time. Ron was cute and funny and he looked out for Cathy. Both came from dysfunctional alcoholic homes. Ron had a car and a job working at his uncle's convenience store, and indulged Cathy with gifts and lots of attention. Since Cathy's parents were virtually useless, she depended on Ron's guidance through the social, emotional, and financial quagmires of adolescence and she adored him. Cathy married Ron when she was 18 and they had their first child when she was 19, and then a second child when she was 20. From that point on Cathy grew up fast, and both of them were overwhelmed. Ron had not advanced very far in his career. He'd tried taking some courses at the community college, but he was never very confident as a student, and the workday and family chores kept him too exhausted. He dropped out. Cathy, on the other hand, did complete her Associate's Degree by working at it part time after her kids started school. Now she was 28, not a kid anymore, she had an Associate's Degree, and Ron, now 38, was still kicking around in unrewarding, dead-end jobs. All illusion was gone.

*Cathy was frustrated and critical of Ron's profes-
sional stagnation. She became frustrated and con-
temptuous of Ron's failures. The old game of "I'm the
good dad and you're the little girl and I'm going to
take care of you," which had worked for both of
them for a while, had given way to two new games.
Hers was called, "I'm the success and you're the burden that I have to put up with." And his was called,
"F%#$ you, b&^*&. I'm going to start hanging out
with some young women who appreciate me, and
you'll never even know about it!"*

When this happens in a marriage it would be beneficial
for the partners to seek professional help.

Chemistry (The Chemical Kind)

In her book *Why We Love*, Helen Fisher describes the
roles of the neurochemicals dopamine, norepinephrine, and
serotonin in impelling us toward relationship, and the
chemicals vasopressin and oxytocin in maintaining our attachment bonds. Dopamine, Fisher reports, helps us to
choose our partners from among the many potential partners available. It also focuses us on the pursuit of our sweetheart, energizes our striving to win love, and correlates with
rising levels of testosterone, "the hormone of sexual desire"
in both men and women; norepinephrine contributes to the
feelings of romantic love such as "exhilaration, excessive energy, sleeplessness, and loss of appetite"; and serotonin is

53

associated with the obsessiveness that characterizes infatuation and the early stages of romantic love. Vasopressin, in men, and oxytocin, in women, contribute to the less dramatic but more durable processes of bonding and attachment.

All of these hormonal dynamics explode onto the scene as we reach puberty, and wreak havoc with the best laid plans of parents to keep kids focused on their futures. Teenagers are notoriously obsessed with the opposite sex, and will often display outrageous ingenuity in "courting and sparking" romantic partners. Remember that history's most famous "starstruck lovers," Romeo and Juliet, were only around 15 when their passions so upset the Montagues and Capulets of medieval Verona.

Recent research suggests that the adolescent brain is not yet fully developed, and won't be until the individual is in his or her early twenties. The adolescent brain lacks some of the capabilities to fully organize a responsible life, such as the ability to delay gratification, to plan for the future, and to show good judgment. Superimpose the compelling biochemical transmutations of love onto the still immature brain of our frisky, irresponsible adolescents, set them free in our open, anything-goes culture, and we've got a powerful set of conditions for creating pairings that make no sense at all. Clearly, for those afflicted at that juncture, "making sense" is far from the point. Evolution seems to have provided us with a sure-fire method of keeping the babies coming as a strategy for survival of our species. The ideals of long term marriage and individual happiness may not be very well integrated into the plan, especially after the survival benefits of shared parenting to the newborn diminishes as the child grows older. So, when a 17-year-old believes that she can marry and live happily ever after with Arrow, the impressively pierced drummer for the band Curling Iron, we can sympathize with her unrealistic optimism, but we can also be forgiven for panicking, and for making every effort to prevent her potentially grave mistake (at least until Arrow gets a day job).

Reading about biochemistry could easily convince us that we humans are no more in control of our behaviors than other members of the animal kingdom. We don't have any trouble accepting that the lifelong bonding of Canadian geese is based in "instinct" and biochemistry. Maybe we're no different, simply differently shaped surging, pumping systems of bio-electrical-chemical impulses, complicated by the injection of cognition and barely channeled through the filters of culture to make new humans. It can easily appear as though we are just another experiment by God or Nature to test the limits of innovation in strategies for survival.

We haven't been very successful in tweezing out the influences of nature and nurture in determining our defining human behaviors, but we do know that they're both in the mix somewhere. This is why transcendence requires so much effort and intention in the individual lives of Marital Artists. Which brings us back to the event we call "falling in love."

Back to Falling

There are few human experiences so powerful as the feelings associated with falling in love. If there were, then probably most of the poetry, stories, books, tv, movies, and songs in the history of the world would never have been written. The artistic attempts at understanding these emotions give us many models, metaphors, and pieces of advice. "Surrender," "fight," "love is grand," "love is a tender trap," it's "all you need," it's "an illusion," it's a "burning deep inside," it's "witchcraft," and on and on.

Many of us, demonstrating the triumph of denial over experience, believe we can marry for love, as in, "they fell in love and lived happily ever after." Way too often it's, "They fell in love and stayed together until they fell out of love and then they limped along for a while making each other miserable until they split." This is almost inevitable if the "love" we're talking about is completely limited to the heady love-rush that gets us in. Experience, and now, even science, tells us that the love-rush can't be sustained. Now what do we do? Flirt, date, date for a long time, be friends, have sex, have a lot of sex, cohabitate, meet the family, accompany each other to social events, take vacations together, but marry??? Why?

Without art, the crudeness of reality would make the world unbearable.
—*George Bernard Shaw*

Chapter 4 What's the Point?

*The journey of transcendence is perilous and diffi-
cult. Take a companion.*
–Chi Shing Chen

*Two are better than one; because they have a good
reward for their labor. For if they fall, the one will
lift up his fellow; but woe to him that is alone when
he falleth, and hath not another to lift him up. Again,
if two lie together, they have warmth; but how can
one be warm alone?*
–Ecclesiastes 4:9-12

Ancient wisdom has always recognized the difficulty of
the journey of life. As individuals we crave partnership and
community. We have, no doubt, inherited this propensity
from our simian predecessors who tend to band together in
social groups. Our human tendency to parley our initial attachments into strong interpersonal bonds and, further, into
complex communities with rich and varied cultures is close
to the essence of who we are. The idea of marriage addresses
our human bonding proclivity.

Some form of institutionalization of marital commitment
seems to have evolved in every culture. This institutionalized

commitment serves societies by stabilizing the rearing of children, ensuring the orderly passage of property from one generation to the next, and formalizing and controlling the potentially chaotic vicissitudes of sexual desire. In her book *Marriage, A History*, Stephanie Coontz spoke of many reasons why people traditionally got married. She said, "Marriage was once part of the credentialing process that people had to go through to gain adult responsibility and respectability." Today, there are other criteria by which we assess "maturity," often related to economic markers, civic and vocational responsibilities, property and ownership of goods, and care-taking of children (unrelated to marriage), and elders. Coontz describes another important historical reason for marriage: the extension of kinship bonds for economic, social, and security reasons. These days mobility has increased to such an extent that many people no longer live in the towns where they were born and extended families and marital kinship bonds have played a shrinking role in the day-to-day social and economic lives of most people. Modern "networking" involves connections that spread far beyond "family," making the establishment of kinship bonds less critical.

Coontz points out that in these times there are a great many circumstances mitigating against marriage in Western cultures. More than ever before people are choosing to cohabitate without the *inconvenience* of marriage vows or marriage ceremonies. More and more children are born outside of marriage and to single mothers. In Western societies the elimination, or at least the liberalization of laws that relegated women to the status of men's property, their greater economic leverage, and the diminishing stigma of "single" status, have made women less dependent on men. Western societies have become much more accepting of alternative living arrangements, from singleness, to gay relationships, to roommates, to group arrangements. Marriage is just not what it used to be. So maybe it's something else.

Linda J. Waite and Maggie Gallagher argue in *The Case for Marriage* that marriage is a good lifestyle choice today. They report, based on their findings, that on the whole, evidence indicates that marriage improves both physical and mental health; marriage improves financial security for both men and women; marriage improves parenting; marriage increases happiness; and marriage is good for sex. Okay, so they say.

Well then how do *we* think about the purpose of marriage in *today's* world and in *our* lives? We understand the purpose of joining a theater troupe: it is to put on a production. We understand the purpose of joining a baseball team: it is to compete and to win games or to have fun and drink beer. What is the purpose of a marriage? Here are some of the answers I get when I ask my clients this question: for love, for companionship, to share a life together, to grow old together... good reasons to spend time together, but, really, all of these things can be done without the commitment of marriage.

One of the more frequently cited purposes of marriage is to have and raise children. In a May 13, 2009, New York

Times article by Gardiner Harris citing data from the Centers for Disease Control and Prevention, it was reported that in the United States in 2007, 4 out of every 10 babies was born outside of a marriage. It is not too surprising that most births to teenagers (86% in 2007) are non-marital, but 60% of births to women 20–24 and nearly one-third of births to women 25–29 occurred outside of marriage as well. Harris reports that the trend is toward more rather than fewer babies born outside of marriage in the future. So, as a reason for getting married, having children seems to be less compelling than it used to be. Even if people did get married in order to have children, it would not provide much of a guarantee that the marriages would be fulfilling to the partners or that they would last. There is evidence to the contrary, specifically, that the arrival of children increases stress and decreases the time that partners have for the relationship (Heaton, 1990; Waite and Lillard, 1991). This is not to say that children can't bring joy to a marriage, but partners would do well to develop strategies for nurturing their relationship because if children are the purpose of a marriage, then it also must be understood that children suffer when marriages go bad. There is evidence that divorce does have a negative effect on children (Cherlin, Chase-Lansdale, & McRae, 1998; McLanehan & Sandefur, 1994), and that, although non-abusive, unhappy marriages are *less* destructive to kids than divorce, they are still not optimal (Waite, L.J., et al, 2002)

"What's love got to do with it?" Does "love" represent a good purpose for making the marriage commitment? Is love enough? It seems to be the answer given most when people are asked why they would marry. "All you need is love," said the Beatles' John Lennon. But the notion of love as starry-eyed infatuation, may not be all you need, at least to extend marriage beyond the seven-year itch. Is "love" really a sufficient reason to marry? Maybe we could think about "love" as necessary but not sufficient. And maybe we need to think about what kind of "love" we're talking about anyway.

The Stanford Encyclopedia of Philosophy defines a variety of kinds of love. The first is *eros,* which is primarily thought of as a passionate desire for the loved one. It's that hot, sexy love that gets everyone in so much trouble. It depends on qualities such as beauty, wealth, power, grace, humor, or what have you, of the loved person, and a desire to acquire those qualities. In relationship terms, this kind of love gets us in deep and fast. It is obsessive and intoxicating and can bring us to the heights of rapture and to the depths of despair before we even know what hit us. It is a very spicy dish, but it's questionable whether it contributes to the sustaining and nourishing value of a long-term relationship or marriage.

A second type of love is *agape,* or brotherly love. This kind of love is unconditional; it doesn't matter what qualities the other person has; it doesn't need to be earned. There are no judgments, no conditions. It's the kind of love that a good parent has for her infant, or that some people believe God and the Saints have for mankind. In an *agape* relationship, we act toward the other person in a loving way regardless of their virtues or inadequacies. This type of love is what we wish for in the way of human relations around the world. And we would like to think that we will love our partners at least as well as we love the rest of our fellow humans, but as a basis for a long-term committed partnership it might be a little emotionally flat for most tastes, and it ignores the insistent dynamics of attraction.

A third type of love discussed by the philosophers is *philia,* which might be described as similar to *eros* but without the sex. You may have *philia* love for a friend, or a business partner or a pet, because of the valuable qualities that they have. Without the sex....? That's probably not going to work in most marriages.

More recently, philosophers have been adding other dimensions to their explorations of "love." Is love about the *Union,* the *Us*? Are we to submerge ourselves into an all-encompassing, loving "Us" so that the two autonomous individuals actually disappear? Love is here defined as a merging of *all* wants and needs. Maybe a little radical for most modern tastes, focused as we are on independence and self-sufficiency.

Or, some philosophers suggest, maybe love is really about expression of a total concern for the beloved; a selflessness that compels us to behave in the other's interests regardless of the costs to ourselves. In this view, the love feelings come from an identification with the well-being of the beloved. This one has difficulties as well. "What about me?" asks a modern partner oriented toward self-actualization, equality and justice.

Another view revolves around valuing the beloved and there seem to be two ways that we can do this. We can "appraise" the value of the beloved and love him or her because we determine that he or she is worthy of our love by virtue of being beautiful, kind, generous, successful, etc. We "respect" such a person, so therefore we may love him or her for *him- or herself* and not merely as a means to our own ends. Alternatively, we can "bestow" value on our beloved by virtue of our loving that person, that is, I love you, so therefore you become valuable to me. In a way, there is a creative component to this approach as opposed to reacting to qualities that already exist. This may interfere with our sense of romance, but we often love our pets in this way, not because they do anything in particular to deserve it.

Another approach involves seeing love as an *emotion complex*. It is a form of "emotional interdependence" that is more than a simple emotional *reaction*. It consists of duration and history and an ability to tolerate, and even embrace, transformation and change. It involves a mutual empathy, and an ability to "enter the other person's point of view." This description represents the kind of love that reflects the values of the Marital Artist, because it is consistent with an appreciation of shared experience, of mutuality and of process. We not only *feel* love, but we *behave in a loving way* that implies an ongoing connection and a commitment to each person's essential right to count all the time. It is not only a *feeling* of love, but an *expression* of love through action; a commitment to share the tasks of creating a life together in a demanding world.

The role of marriage in history has always involved some very practical aspects. Many of the historical benefits of marriage enumerated by Stephanie Coontz in *Marriage: A History* still exist. But in addition to these, modern Marital Artists must create a set of personal "meanings" and purposes that will sustain them in their marriage; transcendent meanings that Linda Waite and Maggie Gallagher describe this way, "[Marriage...represents] the choice to enter that uniquely powerful and life enhancing bond that is larger and more durable than the immediate, shifting feelings of two individuals."

So, because we don't really need to be married to live together, or to have sex or babies, or share money, vacations, friends... And we don't want to lock each other up; stifle; limit; restrict... we need to find a purpose for our marriage that suits our largest vision of our lives; a purpose worthy of our transcendent strivings.

On the other hand, it's hard to imagine that any "purpose" is grand enough to make the marital commitment worthwhile if we hold the belief that marriage is impossible or hopeless and untenable! Let's try to confront this question honestly. We're a fickle, self-centered lot with tiny attention spans. Our culture revolves around ephemeral fashions, music, TV shows, news cycles and video games. We're not used to making commitments that are likely to last more than a season, never mind a lifetime.

How long do you expect your car to last? How long would you *want* it to last? What if you knew that once you bought it you would have it *forever*; even if it broke down? Even if your needs change? No switching to a van when the kids come, or a little red sports car during the mid-life crisis. No Ferrari after you win the lottery.

What about food? Would you really want to eat the same meal every day? How about wearing the same clothes? Can we even imagine getting to a golden anniversary? Fifty years with the same person? One other single, imperfect, aging every day, leaves the dishes in the sink, dries underwear in the shower, person? Whoaaaa.

We understand that we never start out with these concerns. In the beginning it's love, the symphony of the angels, out of your mind, floating on a cloud, walking into walls, blind with passion. Bathed in a marinade of optimism, hope, and denial, we are insulated from doubt. Can two people, coming together in this biochemical fog of infatuation and lust, find their way to a worthwhile, soul-enhancing life together?

Joan and Alan were so besotted with each other when they met in college that they couldn't see straight. They had so much to talk about. They had passionate, creative, and tender sex. They couldn't keep their hands off each other, and their friends would constantly roll their eyes in a confused mix of admiration and repulsion at their public displays of affection. They married after graduation and had their first child while Alan was in business school. Life became more tense as responsibilities mounted. School, a second child, money, Joan's frustration at deferred plans for her own continued education... Then there were some in-law problems and an issue with a learning delay in their first child. Bickering ignited into raging arguments. Joan began to believe that Alan's "ambition" was becoming an obsession, that he had abandoned his family and was neglecting his responsibilities to his son's special needs, not to mention her need for help around the house and her craving for emotional support and affection. Alan felt that Joan was being demanding and unsupportive in his new and very stressful job with a promising new company. He felt that Joan had no interest in his exciting projects. He had tried suggesting, subtly, he thought, that he did not find Joan's extra weight (never lost after the second baby was born) attractive. By the time Alan had his affair with a lovely and witty accountant at work, the relationship was already hopelessly mired in distrust, resentment, disappointment, frustration, hurt and rage. Alan had already decided to move in with the accountant when Joan guilt-tripped him into attending counseling "for the sake of the kids." He resisted any suggestions for focusing attention on his moribund marriage and two months later Joan and Alan were separated on the way to divorce.

Are too many married people, like Joan and Alan, destined to emerge from their honeymoon bliss to stagger through the phases of home building and baby-making only to arrive at an acrimonious divorce after years of disappointment, frustration, anger, and loneliness? Why do they do it? Is there any hope that a marriage can be sustained without sucking the vital life forces right out of our souls and leaving us to proceed as stiff legged and sallow-eyed soldiers of the marital Zombie brigade?

It's not impossible! We can do it, and we're going to see how. Spending time with each other doesn't have to be like eating the same meal over and over again, or like driving the same car because we don't have to be the same people, day after day. We have the ability to continually reinvent ourselves, just like a painter who starts with the same materials but creates new "art" every day.

Every time we have a new thought, read a book, watch a movie, take a trip, plan a meal, engage with friends, take a course, change a job or a house, rearrange the furniture, change our hair or clothes, our routines, emerge from a meditation, prayer or exercise session, or experience a million other changes, we change. We can be as interesting and as varied as we want to be. By thinking about our infinite capacity to transform ourselves we are liberated from the drab and terrifying prospect of repeating the stultifying rituals of life, the same way, every day, with the same person.

In the movie Groundhog Day, weatherman Phil Connors is condemned to repeat every day, the same as the day before, until he is struck by the epiphany that by transforming his outlook, he can extricate himself from this endless, repetitive loop. It's an incredibly liberating notion. Change something in the routine of your life, in the pattern of your thinking or your behavior, and you change your life. Now you have one of the fundamental secrets to turning your life and your marriage into "art."

Another reason that marriages can work is that for many of us, our motivation to belong to something larger than ourselves is strong and deep. Even in our individualistic Western world many of us yearn to subsume ourselves in a group, a club, a political party, a team, to share values, beliefs, and goals with someone other than ourselves. This motivation can be channeled to help us maintain our commitment to the process of marriage. Even when the process is bumpy.

We also get a big boost from Mother Nature. We are designed by God or nature (some of us more and some of us less), through the mystical processes of evolution, to bond to one another, to want to maintain some constancy in our deep intimate connections. Scientific explorations, as discussed above, are beginning to identify some of the specific chemistry that contributes to our bonding proclivities, but for our purposes right now, we can just be grateful that this innate capacity to bond can become the pedestal, or the easel upon which the Marital Art rests while we do our creative work.

So why do we marry? According to Kabbala, the compulsion to rush into a lifelong commitment is an expression of the human soul's deepest ambitions. The subliminal signals emanating from the soul have caused the logic-defying institution of marriage to be an integral part of the human fabric since the dawn of time. The soul's desire to connect and commit makes the aspiration for marriage one of our most basic instincts.

Whereas bodily needs and tendencies are decidedly egocentric, the soul is totally selfless. Commitment without the expectation of a commensurate return benefit may sound absurd when talking the language of the body, but is music to the ears of the soul. The soul's most fervent wish is to transcend itself. Marriage offers the soul the opportunity to express its altruistic nature.

Marriage is about two souls who put their individual needs aside, and commit themselves 100% to the success of the relationship.

(From the Chabad-Lubavitch website chabad.org)

The assessment above implies that the purpose of marriage – to encourage and support transcendence of the soul – is natural, worthwhile, and possible. That's encouraging. But in our times we also often think of our lives in more inclusive secular, carnal, and material terms. To "transcendence of the soul" we could add the following: we make the *commitment* of marriage in order to help each other create the best lives we can. The idea of the "best" life is very open to creative interpretation. The "best" life is whatever my partner and I say it is: the best life spiritually, of course, striving for transcendence of the soul if that is our value, but also, the best life morally, physically, sexually, financially, as parents, as grandparents, as friends, as playmates, as thinkers, as members of the community. Such a commitment abounds with possibilities. But it also implies a demanding set of responsibilities. It is romantic and exciting, but it is also humbling and perhaps intimidating. If kept with integrity, this commitment can raise us to the highest levels of transcendence and fulfillment in many areas of our lives, and actualize our creative visions for ourselves. It can be the foundation for Marital Art.

Before I end this section I would like us to keep in mind that not everyone chooses to make the commitment of marriage. These are always very personal decisions, and are entitled to our fullest respect. Some people just want to be alone, not because they are losers or that they think marriage is impossible, but simply because they don't feel that it is for them. These people may feel that it is not the right time, that they need to be free, that they haven't met the right person, that they are focusing on career goals, that they don't want the responsibility or the commitment, or they quite courageously are willing to admit that they want to focus on themselves, that they aren't financially secure enough, that they are too young, too lost or confused, too damaged from previous relationships or from emotional injuries stemming from childhood. People who say that they are not ready for a commitment should be trusted, and left alone until they *are* ready. They can continue to be great friends, but they are not going to be good marriage partners until they are ready to be marriage partners. If you are putting energy into convincing someone that he or she should marry you, don't bother. Neither of you will be happy if you succeed.

Blessed are they who see beautiful things in humble places where other people see nothing.
—Camille Pissarro

Chapter 5 Developing Your Craft

The wise man knows that some day even the sun's light and warmth will be gone and that we will cease to be. And yet, he still builds a house.
–Chi Shing Chen

God, grant me serenity to accept the things I cannot change;
Courage to change the things I can;
And wisdom to know the difference.
–Reinhold Niebuhr, Serenity Prayer

Artists must build basic skills and develop the craft that will allow them to be expressive in the manner that reflects their highest artistic aspirations. A painter does figure studies, a musician does scales, a baseball player takes batting practice. Marital Artists understand that a relationship is an ensemble, and marriage is a collaborative art. If you were going to join a Shakespearian stage production, you would need to prepare rigorously for the challenge of being part of the troupe. Anyone who has ever participated in a group effort, performed in theater, taken part in an orchestra, played on a team, collaborated on a work, church, temple, or political committee, understands that the extent to which you serve the ensemble depends on the extent to which you have personally prepared and honed the basic skills of the enterprise, and the extent to which you practice. Before you can hope to contribute to a performance on the stage, you must know the basics of characterization, stage movement, voice projection, taking direction, hitting your marks, etc. Before joining an orchestra you must know how to play your instrument, read music, follow the conductor, modulate your sound, etc. To play on a baseball team you need to develop the skills of catching fly-balls, and grounders, throwing with speed and accuracy, hitting, running bases, remembering signals, anticipating the intentions of opposing players, etc.

To make it in the "marital ensemble" it helps to have some useful skills, some personal and some interpersonal.

Useful Personal Skills

Attending to the demons left over from our early development and the ones we pick up along the way

We all need to be able to identify the demons that sabotage our best intentions in order to be good marital partners. There are usually more than one. Pettiness? Laziness? Rage? Greed? Selfishness? Manipulativeness? Passivity? Impatience? Self-righteousness? Vindictiveness? Indecisiveness? Sloth? Bossiness? Sloppiness?... More? How about Drinking? Gambling? Lying? Promiscuity? Gluttony?

These demons are especially problematic for the aspiring Marital Artist, because they disrupt our ability to keep our deals. How can we keep our promise to love when we have no control over our rage, abusive mouth, or violence? For that matter, how can we make a deal to show up to meet for tennis if we're drunk? People who can't control themselves can't keep their deals and their partners are going to be distrustful and resentful. To summarize so far: Demons ruin deals. Ruined deals lead to distrust. Distrust leads to.... let's just say, big problems.

Being aware of your shifting needs and wants

The young lover believes that there is no love without incense and lotus blossoms. With experience she understands that love does not require incense or lotus blossoms. Though they are nice.
–Chi Shing Chen

We often think of ourselves in terms of needs. Needs just are. "I need air to breath." "I need understanding." "I need new kitchen cabinets before the graduation party."

Psychologist Abraham Maslow described a hierarchy of needs that begins with the need for safety and basic biological sustenance, and proceeds through the need for love, to self-actualization.

What happens if we don't get what we need? The consequences can range from failure to achieve self-actualization and transcendence, through some version of failure to thrive, through minimally acceptable survival, to death. Relationships have their own potential list of consequences when the relationship needs are not met. The consequences of sustained periods of unmet needs are resentment, frustration, anger, emotional distance, and ultimately, dissolution of the relationship. Not exactly what we signed up for. Why would anyone stay in a relationship with someone if needs aren't being met? You wouldn't continue to patronize an auto mechanic who failed to meet your needs:

"Why did you put avocados in where the spark plugs are supposed to be?"
"Um, I didn't have any spark plugs."
"Oh, OK. I need new brakes too. Can you take care of that for me?
"Well, I don't have any break pads, but I can throw on a coupl'a slices of cheese."
"Great. Let me know when you're done."

I don't think so. But who knows, maybe that customer really, *really* wanted the wacky mechanic to like him and fixing the car was just a secondary need. Well, it happens, and for a variety of other reasons as well. If someone is staying in a relationship then some need *is* being met even though it may not look like it. "What could she possibly see in *him*?" Sometimes it's not obvious.

Partners, especially those from dysfunctional families of origin, often don't know what they need. They invest in chaos and abuse and never get the mind-body-and-soul-enhancing treatment that they really need in order to flourish. They have developed strategies to achieve the barest levels of survival, which are grossly inadequate to achieve a thriving, transcendent, and self-actualized life, not to mention satisfaction in their relationships. Often they don't have the self-esteem required to understand that they are entitled to pursue life-affirming treatment in their relationships, and they are willing to settle for a rougher approximation of relationship, or a certain level of material well-being in order to avoid what to them seem the terrifying alternatives of isolation, loneliness, or impoverishment. Maybe, because of the inadequate nurturance of their childhood experience, this is the tragic, primitive level of their needs, simply not to feel isolated and alone or lacking a roof and a meal. They will put up with almost anything else.

Willard F. Harley in his 1986 book *His Needs, Her Needs*, describes some very gender specific needs that may seem outdated from our current perspective, a third of a century later. He says that a man seeks gratification of these "needs" from his partner:

1. Sexual fulfillment

2. Recreational companionship

3. An attractive spouse

4. Domestic support

5. Admiration

while a woman "needs":

1. Affection

2. Conversation

3. Honesty and openness

4. Financial support

5. Family commitment

Before we giggle and write this list of "needs" off as quaint, sexist, and dated, we have to acknowledge that some of us will shake our heads in agreement, "yes, that pretty much sums it up for me." Some of us, of each gender will say, "ummm, nah. Not me."

Men Are from Mars, Women Are from Venus by John Gray, also argues that there are specific gender differences, based on biology and culture that color some of the essential needs of men and women. For instance, the author writes that women want frequent acknowledgement of a loving relationship status, gestures and words reflecting affection and positive regard, while men want recognition for the efforts they make, the things they do, and the esteem that these actions reflect. He says that men and women keep score of the relationship based on these different need systems.

I think that it is less useful to seek broad generalizations that describe all of us all the time, than to understand, as psychologist Abraham Maslow suggested, that the salience of specific needs is reconfiguring all the time. Kind of like a game of Whack-a-Mole. Whack-a-mole is an arcade game where you spot a pesky mole sticking its head out of a hole and you whack it with a mallet and then another mole pops up and you whack *it*, pretty much forever and you gain points on the basis of how effectively you dispatch the critter that's confronting you. If we are dehydrated to the point of dizziness then money, sex, and affection recede in their importance for both sexes. Let's "whack" thirst by getting something to drink. But once you've been watered, you may start to feel the need for affection, sex, or for something else, perhaps a trampoline in the backyard. There are probably wide individual variations in specific needs (such as those outlined by Harley), and trying to divide them up by gender may not the best way to think about them. I would suggest, with Maslow, that it may be more productive to think in terms of an ever shifting field of "needs" (or moles).

Aspiring to meet our own needs as well as those of others – those of our partners, children, co-workers, friends, homes, cars, pets – can often make us feel like whacking moles is a full time job.

So much of the difficulty that arises in relationships concerns our perceptions of needs, both ours and our partners, and our expectations regarding the gratification of those needs.

Kathy felt that she and Jim needed a romantic getaway in order to reconnect. She was feeling distant and resentful of their insane schedules and the demands of everything and everyone around them. They barely saw each other in the mornings and evenings long enough to discuss kids and bills.
Jim felt that he and Kathy needed a new deck in the yard, so that they could have a place to share the

peace and quiet of a glass of wine on warm spring
and summer evenings after a typically stressful day.
"If we don't get out of here soon, I'm going to ex-
plode," said Kathy.
"If we blow our savings on a trip, we'll get home and
be back in the stress pit within a week. A deck is for-
ever," countered Jim.
They both felt the need to reconnect, but their pre-
scriptions for the solution to the problem created
conflict.

It is useful to evaluate our attitudes and values regarding our needs and those of our partners. Who is responsible for the satisfaction of whose needs? Am I responsible for your clean socks? Are you responsible for my orgasm? Whose responsibility is it to make sure that we each feel loved and safe and trusted? The Marital Artist understands that the effective negotiation of these responsibilities is among the fundamental processes of the relationship.

Unfortunately, we often enter a relationship with our own sets of rules regarding these responsibilities, rules absorbed from the processes of functioning (or "dis" functioning) manifested in our families of origin. For instance, in one home it may be assumed that men take out the garbage and women clean the toilets; a woman brings a man a drink after he's had a hard day at work; a man works as many jobs as he needs to in order to keep his wife and family in an acceptable lifestyle; an angry person mopes and grumbles and tosses things around until somebody asks, "What's the matter?"

Sometimes our expectations of entitlements and obligations are unjust and unfair but they are deeply held. At a deep emotional level we expect our needs to be met in ways that have been informed by the processes of our families of origin. You'll treat me like a princess because my Daddy did. You'll keep things organized for me because that's what Mommy did. (Or, sometimes.... "You'll protect me because Daddy didn't." or, "You'll make me feel valued because Mommy didn't." It can go either way.) But, whatever our need-expectations coming into a marriage, we are often in for a rude awakening when we discover that our partners have a different set of rules and expectations. These "rules" are often so unconscious and ingrained, so metaphysically assumed and unexamined that we can't imagine that our partner, this person with whom we are bound in love and life, could ever hold a different view. Therefore, when they don't "go along" it must be because they are being obstinate, inconsiderate, and selfish; or because they hate us or are just mean. (These may be the conclusions that would have been drawn from our family-of-origin experience.)

Eventually, when a shared concept of the "rules" eludes us, we employ strategic interventions to get our needs met. In the worst cases, partners maneuver to get what they perceive to be their needs met in underhanded or manipulative ways. In the best of cases there is a natural, often unspoken, complimentarity in meeting each other's needs. Marital Artists not only understand that it works when we scratch each other's backs, but it works even better when I scratch your head and you scratch my back if that's where we itch. The dance of need gratification depends on a graceful movement in and out of personal and shared responsibility for ourselves and each other. The Marital Artist understands that the dance goes smoothly when we communicate and maintain a rhythm rooted in our love and trust, an understanding that "we both count all the time," and an awareness that our happiness is linked to the happiness of our beloved. People who speak "functional relationship" as a primary language absorbed from functional family-of-origin experience have a distinct advantage. Those who are not so lucky, and who have experienced ineffective or dysfunctional family process, must strive to learn functionality as a second language. We all know how much harder it is to learn a second language later in life, after the optimal language acquisition windows are closed, but it certainly can be done. Either way, the Marital Artist keeps in mind the fundamental purpose of the marriage, that we are here to help each other have the best life we can have.

Know Thyself

The philosopher said, "Know thyself." Good advice if you are a solo act, but also quite essential for partners in a relationship. Self awareness is a most important personal skill. Without knowing our wants and fears, hopes and dreams, it is hard to be intentional about our actions. We will lack purpose and direction, we will not know what to pursue and what to leave behind. We will not know what to ask for, and we will not know when we want to say, "no." Relationships depend on our ability to make deals, and knowing ourselves, especially our needs and wants, is an essential prerequisite to making good deals.

"Knowing ourselves," like the acquisition of most other skills, begins with an intention. Pay attention. Your being gives you information all the time. We always want some things, and don't want others. We want things (cars, jewelry, a Caesar salad), we want states of mind (happiness, peace, love), we want specific interpersonal transactions (foot rub, kindness, sex, understanding, listening). We don't want other things (the anchovy banana crunch ice cream, the polka-dot cardboard siding); we don't want other states of mind (sadness, anger, loneliness); we don't want other inter-personal transactions (a punch in the face, a lie, a cold shoulder). We can learn to know that we want or don't want these, and many other specific things, by tuning into our-selves, opening up and refraining from judging the informa-tion that we get. Let's think about that: Wants cannot be judged. It is easy to get confused about this. We can become very judgmental about wants. "How can you want that? You're disgusting (stupid, weak, greedy, insensitive, uni-maginative, etc)." But if we want to encourage ourselves and our partners to be honest about our desires, we must be open to all kinds of possibilities. On the other hand, actions can and should be judged. The well-being of the community that is our marriage depends on anticipating the implications of our wants for our partner, and our taking responsibility for our actions.

In order to proceed through our lives, and to function effectively in our relationships, we have to know what we want. But we don't always have to satisfy these wants. I suppose that part of being a grownup is acceptance of the idea that we cannot get everything we want. Often we will choose not to pursue a want because it is in conflict with some other want: "I want to watch TV instead of practicing the piano, but I also want to be a good piano player." Sometimes our wants conflict with our values: "I want to drop my empty coffee container on the ground rather than carry it around, but I value a clean community." Sometimes our wants conflict with the wants of our partner: "I want a lazy evening at home; my partner wants a night out on the town."

As Mick Jagger said, "You can't always get what you want," but if you try real hard you might find that if you know what you want, and if you have a partner who cares about your wants, you might be able to get more, rather than less, of your wants satisfied. As a Marital Artist, it helps to know what both you and your partner want so that you can help both of you get more of it. Developing awareness of what you want and what your partner wants, finding an equilibrium between them, knowing what to pursue and what to let go, are among the important skills practiced by Marital Artists.

Maintaining some control over yourself

If you want to be free to be as impulsive and undisciplined as a wood sprite that's great. Go for it. But this approach will make it difficult to maintain a marriage with anyone who is not a saint, or who has any modicum of self-respect. Indulging another person's lack of discipline becomes very tiring after a while.

Martial artists understand that being able to perform under pressure requires intensive training in self-discipline. Without self-discipline we react to circumstances in an impulsive, disorganized manner which often manifests as panic, chaos, inefficient short cuts, lack of, or half-hearted effort, disengagement, lack of concentration, follow-through, or focus, poor performance, or self-indulgence.

Remember that being a Marital Artist requires a recognition and awareness that both you and your partner count all the time, even when you are tired, hungry, horny, lazy, angry, bitter, needy, or "not in the mood." Coping with the complex variety of our inner states and maintaining our focus on the marriage and the well-being of our partner is at the core of the Marital Art.

For most of us this is one of the most difficult aspects of marriage. It requires full-time commitment and intention to maintain self-discipline. We must grow into it. The "inner child" in all of us would prefer that our partner forgive us, pick up the slack, "lighten up", "get over it", in general, indulge and patronize our failures of self-discipline. Maybe they will. But if we are depending on their ability to consistently perform the role of "good daddy or mommy," indulgent, forgiving, picking up after our messes, we are not developing our Marital Art. (Maybe they are, but again, if they have any self-respect they are going to get tired of it.)

Maintaining effective stress management skills

Life is stressful. Marriage is stressful. The creation of art in any field presupposes an ability to de-stress, or "center," so that artistic performance is optimal. Imagine a singer stepping out on the stage in front of thousands and being too stressed to hit the first note. This is not to say that performance does not benefit from a level of excitement, or readiness. There is an inherent and positive value in "motivating" stress, or as it is technically called, "eustress." This is the stress that we feel when we are inspired to be at our best. It is energizing and impels us to positive action.

The kind of stress that we don't need, and that we must develop an ability to manage, is the "distress" which depletes us of energy and corrodes our ability to perform. Often, when stress levels get too high we become disabled, dysfunctional, incapable of performing at the levels to which we aspire. Often, stress makes us regress. When we are having difficulty coping we revert to behavioral strategies that we relied on at a less developed period of our life. We can become dependent, whiny, demanding, self-indulgent, selfish, withdrawn, aggressive, manipulative. We lose our capacity for collaboration and creative problem solving. We become insensitive to the plight of others. We seek soothing solutions for ourselves that don't do anything to resolve our impasses, but provide temporary relief from the oppressive pressures of the current stress. If this strategy works at all, it often does so only temporarily and only for us, often at the expense of our partner or our relationship.

Marital Artists have developed strategies for managing stress by organizing their lives to minimize stress; by developing life skills that mitigate stressful contingencies, and by developing de-stressing practices that modulate personal levels of stress. There is an enormous amount of material written about stress reduction (making life changes, developing new healthful habits, meditating, exercising, sleeping, de-cluttering, shifting attitudes, etc.) and it is beyond the scope of this discussion. But it should be emphasized `that by developing means of managing stress, Marital Artists strengthen the ability to behave with intention and maturity in their relationships, more, rather than less frequently.

Useful Interpersonal Skills

Being trusting and trustworthy

It stands to reason that partners who are trusting and trustworthy are likely to have very few problems with trust in their relationship. We will likely be trusting if we have not been deceived, manipulated, or abused in our current relationship (early childhood, and prior relationship experience will also, most certainly, color our ability to trust). Partners will be perceived as trustworthy to the extent that they do what they say, and follow through with deals, are congruent and transparent in their words and actions, and are considerate and loving in their dealings with each other. Trust is clearly one of the core elements of an "Artistic" marriage and will be discussed in more detail in Chapter 12.

Being able to make and keep deals

Can you make and keep deals? Can you give your word and follow through regardless of what happens later on to change your mind, or what the other guy does or what obstacles pop up to prevent it, or what seductive alternative options emerge after you made the deal? To maintain a functional, not to mention "Artistic" process in a relationship, it doesn't really matter what you agree to, or how pretty your promises sound, if you can't make and keep deals consistently.

Relationships, at their most fundamental level, are about emotional connections that are maintained by the making and keeping of deals. Most of the problems that cripple marriages can often be reduced to dysfunctional deal-making and deal-keeping, starting with the original deal made during the wedding ceremony, which usually includes some variation of the promise to love, honor, and respect. We make this promise at the very first moment of our marriage, and then, if we are not attentive and vigilant, we too often go on to treat our partners un-lovingly, dishonorably, and disrespectfully. Making the right kind of deals and keeping them turns out to be a formidable challenge because we are fallible and it is so easy to lose our focus. Being unable, unwilling, or uncommitted enough to make and keep deals destroys trust and creates deep animosity and resentment that will corrode a marriage. With regard to relationships, the old saying, "A man [woman] is as good as his/her word," states the case pretty succinctly. That said, there are many reasons why deals are broken, some of them beyond our control, and our expectations about our partners must be tempered with some reasonable understanding of human frailty and the "slings and arrows of outrageous fortune." To forgive is divine... But when personal demons, regressed emotional states, lack of focus or inconsiderateness consistently get in the way of our deal-keeping it places a burden on our partners, destroys trust, and stresses the relationship often to the breaking point.

Developing the capacity to manage deal-making and deal-keeping is a fundamental part of the Marital Art. And simple as it appears to be, the discipline required to make and keep deals may be among the most important skills that marital partners can possess. Keeping deals leads to trust.

Maintaining the perspective that everybody counts, even under stress

In the early 15th century, Renaissance painters discovered perspective and revolutionized art. The discovery and exploration of perspective can also revolutionize your marriage. We are born with a narcissistic, self-centered view of the world. A child's world view pretty much boils down to: "It's all about me." As we mature we develop the capacity to empathize with others, to understand their feelings, their hopes, fears, dreams, and pains, their likes and dislikes. This adult interpersonal perspective, allows us to recognize all the ways that we can "come from different places" emotionally and yet enter the river together. Accurate empathy is a valued quality of the Marital Artist. When we don't fall back into childish self-centeredness due to stress, fear, habit, or loss of focus, we can accept that our partner often has a different, and quite reasonable, agenda from us. S/he wants to "get up and go" when we want to crash and recover; s/he wants silence when we want noise; s/he wants sex when we want affection. For the Marital Artist these differences are perceived as starting points of dialogue. They don't necessarily lead to battle. They don't create the inevitability that either your partner or you will be proven "wrong," or that both will go away angry and frustrated, or that one will get his/her way and the other won't, or, that perhaps, everyone will lose. Accepting the perception of difference simply means that in the upcoming discussion, you will be starting from separate, idiosyncratic, personal places until there is a resolution that brings you together in a shared understanding, which is always the goal. Most of the apparent potential conflict that we initially perceive can be reframed by means of perspective and worked out creatively, as long as we don't interpret our differences counter-productively. It is easy to see the other person not as simply different, but as "bad" or "wrong" or "against me." Once we get into this kind of defensive and judgmental territory we are setting ourselves up for polarization and adversarial battle. This can happen easily if we are distracted by stressors, revert to old habits, or lose focus on our intention to create outcomes that work for us both.

The Marital Artist strives to become practiced in the skill of taking the other person's point of view and developing accurate empathy. S/he understands that this does not mean that his/her own point of view doesn't matter. To the contrary, both points of view matter, all the time. The Art lies in integrating both points of view into a solution that works for both. To this end, a process must be employed that is loving, respectful, generous, and fair. We will discuss this process in Chapter 7.

Possessing practiced and effective communication skills

When I see couples in counseling, the first thing they usually tell me is that there is a problem in communication. Communication is a complex art in itself. It involves very important skills which let us bridge the gap between our inner world, and that of our partner. Without skillful verbal and non-verbal communication our constantly transforming inner river of feelings, thoughts, hopes, fears, dreams, wants, observations, perceptions, experiences, memories, and ideas would be bound up inside of each of us with no hope of flowing over the dam. Communication is the part of the art that allows us to connect, to be together, to not be alone, and to share our wants and needs. We will discuss the important topic of communication in more detail in Chapter 10.

Possessing an effective arsenal of fair-play conflict resolution skills

Because we are different people, and because we come to every situation from a different perspective, we often have to resolve the apparent conflicts that arise when our points of view don't align. I refer to these as apparent conflicts, because they don't have to involve adversarial combat, and for the Marital Artist they rarely do. Marital Artists try hard to maintain the position that different points of view are to be expected, respected, and valued, and that resolving these apparent conflicts is going to conclude with both partners feeling okay with the outcome, and more important, okay with the process. They eschew "win at any cost" strategies, and seek preferred "win-win" outcomes. They communicate their wants and their passions in ways that make it possible for their partner's wants and passions to be considered as well. They work in an atmosphere of trust, and strive to minimize defensiveness. They maintain a process that is loving, respectful, and considerate.

The purpose of art is washing the dust of daily life off our souls.
—Pablo Picasso

Chapter 6 Partnership and the Transcendent Journey

I am at the tiller of a small boat, sailing across a vast sea. The winds and tides that came before have brought me here and taught me much. Now, which way shall I go?
–Chi Shing Chen

There is nothing in the caterpillar that lets you know it's going to be a butterfly.
–R. Buckminster Fuller

The Marital Artist understands that marriage to the right person at the right time can provide a transcendent opportunity. It is an opportunity to share the journey of moving above and beyond the accidents of our birth. What are these "accidents" of birth? They include all of the factors that helped to form us, and over which we had no control. These might include our physical attributes, such as skin or hair color; gender; our parents and kin stretching back to the first man and woman; our gifts, such as intellect, judgment, impulse control, empathy, imagination, physical beauty, grace and strength, and personality attributes (need for control, order, curiosity, recognition, attention, intellectual stimulation); our time in history and geographic place on the planet; our social status and wealth; the culture we inherit from our parents and neighbors; our primary language and the way it shapes our thinking; the media we are exposed to; the propaganda and marketing; the illnesses we suffer; the ecological conditions during the time of our development. Clearly, the list can go on and on. And without getting into lofty discussions of free will and determinism, suffice it to say that there is much over which we have no control. There is a time, however, if we are very lucky, that we may become aware of this existential condition and make a conscious decision to transcend it. It is at this point that we can begin to make the efforts to transform our values and reshape ourselves. What a wonderful opportunity this provides for Marital Artists partnering in a marriage: the opportunity for each to help the other transcend the "accidents" of their births and become all that they can be. What are some of the qualities of transcendence to which both contribute, and which emanate from a growthful marriage?

The qualities of transcendence, first of all, reflect an inclusive perspective that comprehends our beginnings in the original accidents of birth (or, if you prefer, the acts of God). This perspective alone helps to free us of both pride and contempt. It contributes to a posture of humility and compassion. We begin to understand that we are all struggling to succeed using the tools we have inherited. Only some of us get to reach beyond this level of existence, those of us *lucky* (or *blessed*) enough to comprehend that we can go further. Either way we understand that we are all trying to do the best we can (or we would do better).

My limited knowledge of the great religious leaders suggests that they all shared qualities of enormous compassion, acceptance, forgiveness, generosity, empathy, and love. Wouldn't it be a worthy goal of our marriages if we could contract to help each other develop these qualities, no matter where we have come from and what experiences have contributed to our development so far?

Building Blocks

All the world is full of suffering. It is also full of overcoming.
–Helen Keller

Many of us spend our days and sleepless nights blaming everything and everybody for our inability to find happiness, and maybe this is the only way that sense can be made of our experience. Some of us are true victims whose misfortune is very much out of our control. We are lied to, beaten, abandoned, or caught in the wrong place at the wrong time. We are born into the wrong family, or the wrong neighborhood, or with the wrong genes, or we suffer terrible accidents or disease; our partner turns out to have a well concealed problem with drugs or alcohol or a family in another state. These things happen, and there's often no way to prevent them. Those of us unfortunate enough to have experienced these tribulations are truly victims. Bad things of varying degrees of magnitude can and will happen to all of us, and we must face the distinct possibility that we could arrive at the end of our lives and say, "I've had a terrible life, and it's all because of ---------."

Or, like Helen Keller, quoted above, we can try to transform ourselves into the people who will be at peace with our choices no matter what the fates have in store. You are truly blessed, indeed, if at the end you can say, "I had a great life, despite ...." How far do you have to go to get there? Well, that depends on where you start.

Here's a hint: You can't start any place but where you are, and it's a good idea to figure out where that is.

I am what I am, and that's all what I am.
–Popeye the Sailor

As mentioned above, philosophers used to advise anyone who would listen to "know thyself." It's a particularly good idea if you're planning to spend your life in a marriage. The more you know about yourself, the more likely you are to make good choices, *for you*, in all areas of your life. What are your strengths and vulnerabilities? What do you want? What are you afraid of? What are your ambivalences? (I want to run a marathon, but running hurts. I want a spouse who's rich, and I also want someone who's playful and easygoing.)

Knowing yourself means understanding what pleases you and what causes pain; it means having the information by which to make good personal choices. Sometimes the way we see ourselves, our *identity*, provides us with an accurate image of our functional strengths and weaknesses and some-

100

times it represents a distortion that causes constant frustration and pain as we interact with our world.

Identity

Our sense of our "self" plays a role in everything we do. Do you see yourself as a success? a problem solver? a victim? a creator? an average Joe or Jane? A doctor, a lawyer, an Indian chief? Our "identities" will inevitably play a significant role in our relationships, even though they are, largely, imaginary.

Part of the narrative that we establish about ourselves involves a story of who we are. It involves our understanding of our history, our development, the important shapers of our destiny; it includes a sense of who we are as physical beings, as economic beings, as romantic and sexual beings, as spiritual beings, as political beings. Our identities include an inventory (accurate or not) of our strengths and weaknesses, of our social capital, of our place in the universe. We develop a sense of who we are as individuals, and as parts of larger entities, our partnerships, our communities, nations, world.

In his book *Childhood and Society*, the great psychologist Erik Erikson described the task of finding "identity" as essential to our successful development and progress through life. He argued that if we don't successfully establish a functional identity somewhere during our adolescent to young adult years, we are condemned to be lost in a fog of "role diffusion," with its inevitable implications of confusion, uncertainty, and a pervasive question of "who am I?"

One's identity is not a simple choice made from a menu of options. It's pretty clear that we do not decide upon an identity at the age of 18 and remain stuck with it for life, even though a lot of "identity searching" is presumed to occur in late adolescence. The process of establishing an identity is probably reflected in the process of picking a major in college (although all of our choices probably reflect our identity). Some of us know exactly what we want to study and be. The rest of us make some tentative decisions and then modify as our options and experience inform our choices. Often our final career trajectories have little or nothing to do with the major we chose in college. This tendency to modify our identities is one of the reasons that an early decision to marry is a risky one. Who knows if we will have the same beliefs, attitudes, values, wants, impulses, and preferences in five, ten, or twenty years? Erik Erikson postulated his theory of identity in a society that was fairly static compared to the one we live in today. It seems that in this rapidly changing world we have to sort through a myriad of ideas, all competing to shape us and color our choices. We have marketing geniuses selling us political, religious, and cultural ideas all the time. It takes longer for people in our postmodern Western cultures to really figure out who they are. We are often works in progress, for a long time, and perhaps the process never ends.

As we learn and experience and grow, we keep refining our sense of ourselves and develop a richer and more complex and nuanced sense of identity and knowing who we are.

Having a strong sense of identity contributes to clarity in the making of our choices. For example, if I think of myself as a pimp, I'll probably choose a different kind of car than I would if I saw myself as an environmental activist.

Another component of identity is who we believe we are in relationship to others. Am I a "loner", am I "the boss," am I kind and affectionate, am I always in control, am I "helpless," am I a "sucker," a "winner," a "fool," am I a team player, a "pushover"? The way we see ourselves in relationship to others will emerge as an important part of our identities, especially in terms of our most important friendships, partnerships, and intimate relationships.

If our identity includes a strong religious faith, it would make sense to choose a partner who shared that faith; likewise with other truly central values. By "central values," I mean those values that stand close to the core of our identities, those that are most important to our sense of ourselves. I will discuss values and attitudes more thoroughly in Chapter 9.

For Marital Artists, being members of the couple is central to their identities. "Let me go check with my honey," they might say when asked to make plans. The first assumption is that they are going to consider the needs and wishes of their partners before making decisions and plans that serve themselves. If they are going to be out later than expected with friends, they'll call home to let their partners know. Their sense of themselves is such that a decision is not going to work unless it also works for their partners. To a significant degree, the answer to the question, "Who am I," is answered by the statement, "I am part of this relationship."

This does not mean that individual wants and needs are disregarded. Rather, it means that both partners take account of each other all the time. They *identify* with each other's well-being. Struggles involve lobbying efforts, which provide information about each person's wants, needs, and feelings on a particular issue. The process emphasizes fair fighting because it is clear to both partners that manipulation will ultimately work against everyone's best interests. Solutions involve the best synthesis of this information and compromises strive for acceptable levels of satisfaction for both. If we each identify strongly with the well-being of the couple then each partner cannot win unless the other wins also, or at least doesn't lose.

Identifying as part of a couple seems to be difficult for many of us, especially those of us who marry later; who have long lists of personal achievements and individual accomplishments; who own a lot of our own stuff; who navigate life with independence and competence. Our "marital identity" must often contend with the seemingly inconsistent realities of prenuptial agreements, partners keeping their own names, maintenance of separate checking, savings, and retirement accounts, subscribing to separate interests, having separate friends, nights out and even vacations. None of these elements of separate identity is a bad thing *per se*, and many serve a useful purpose, but we must keep in mind that the "us" part of our identities requires a certain critical mass before we have enough "marriage" to transform into Marital Art.

A sense of identity as part of a couple does not eliminate conflict, just as an integrated personal identity can leave plenty of room for conflict within ourselves. However, such a sense of identity can provide a guiding structure for the resolution of conflicts.

Mine, Yours and Ours

If we create a diagram of our relationship, we can get an idea of how much of our lives are reserved for ourselves and how much is shared.

Different ways to identify as a couple:

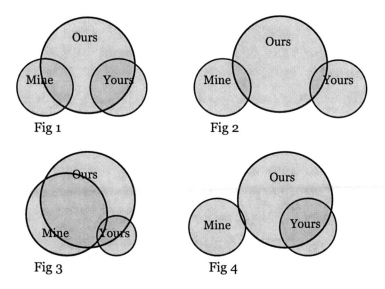

Fig 1

Fig 2

Fig 3

Fig 4

Simply reserving separate space for ourselves does not preclude identity as a couple. However, those who identify as part of the couple work out their own space requirements in conjunction with each other, so that the balance of all elements works for both. There is no one "right" solution and a wide range of variations can work as long as there is an underlying confidence, felt by each partner, that "we both count, all the time." If one of us identifies as "owning" the relationship (Fig 3), or if one of us identifies much more with the relationship than the other (Fig 4), then there will likely be significant problems.

On Being Right

There was once a rabbi who was so open-minded that he could see every side of a question.

One day a man came to visit the rabbi with the request that he grant him a divorce.

"What do you hold against your wife?" asked the rabbi, gravely.

The man went into a lengthy recital of his complaints.

When the man finished, the rabbi shook his head as he stroked his beard and agreed, "You are right."

Then the rabbi turned to the woman.

"Now let us hear your story," he urged.

And the woman in her turn began to tell of the cruel mistreatment she had suffered at her husband's hands.

The rabbi listened with obvious distress.

When she finished, he said with conviction, "You are right."

At this, the rabbi's wife, who was present, exclaimed, "How can this be? First you said he was right, and then you said she was right. Surely they cannot both be right!"

The rabbi knitted his brows and reflected.

"You're right, too!" he agreed.

After Nathan Ausubel, A Treasury of Jewish Folklore

Wherever we come from, somewhere along the line the need to be "right" develops a powerful hold on many of us. It develops from experience. We seek validation of our view of the world. It can be very disorienting to "know" that the bluefish is better on the grill, and have somebody tell you that it would be better baked in the oven with marinara sauce. When this person is your spouse, the person with whom you identify as a couple, it is very disconcerting, indeed. "How can you believe that, when I believe this?" It can feel as though you are being told that your fundamental perceptual capacities are faulty, or that you are deficient, or it can imply that you are not really as together as a couple as you thought you were. "Maybe we *are* incompatible." It can feel like there is a real pressure to make your perceptions converge so that you can once again feel like you are in alignment with each other. Of course each person wants that alignment to happen through support of *his or her* perception. So, we go about the work of convincing each other.

Sometimes being "right" gives a person status and power. If you are "right," you are "one up" on your partner. This enhanced status provides capital that can be used to redeem past humiliations and to provide leverage in future arguments. This manipulative association of "rightness" with status often has roots in our experience, but, as we can see, it works against the Marital Artist's more transcendent goals.

We develop an aversion to being wrong at an early age. We are often chastised or shamed for being wrong, sometimes called names like "stupid" or "moron." When we are "wrong" we earn poor grades and are told that our hopes of a prosperous future will disappear. Sometimes there are punishments involved, fines, loss of status, love, friendship, or esteem. The stakes can be high. We can get pretty attached to the idea of being "right."

Fighting to be right is often unconscious and reflexive, especially if the perceived costs of being wrong are high. The operational idea here is "perceived." Sometimes the stakes *feel* high even when they are not. We imagine that we will lose something if we are wrong. What is that "something"? In retrospect we often can't imagine what was so important about being right. Consider a recent "discussion" by Phil and Janet:

"Carol said the party is going to start at 7."
"No she didn't.
"Yes she did."
"No she didn't."
"Yes she did."

108

What is this argument really about? Why can't they just call Carol? Maybe the time of the party is not really the issue. Sometimes these couples are involved in a transactional game that we can call, "Who's the idiot," because if it's you, then I am not the bad one; or I am one up on you and I gain status and power. Sometimes, as described above, we are certain of our perception and it is uncomfortable not to have our certainty validated.

Most of us don't have any trouble seeing how this compulsion to be right operates in our relationships. We can fight over anything. We can hold passionate opinions:

> "If we don't buy this truckload of sponges now it will mean we've blown the best opportunity we will ever have."
> "You're insane."
> "No, you're insane."
> "You're certifiable."
> "You're a gutless wimp."

The impulse to fight to be right can be so deeply rooted and intractable that it seems impossible to cut it out. I've heard couples argue over one person's assertion of their most personal preferences:

> "I love the chocolate ones."
> "No you don't. You hate the chocolate ones. You never eat the chocolate ones."
> "Yes I do. I love the chocolate ones."
> "You don't either."

Making progress in the battle to give up being "right" is like any other struggle to transcend the petty and infantile elements in our characters. It starts with the will and perhaps a shift in identity. We can work to reconfigure an identity that requires certainty, and is threatened by uncertainty. We can work to develop an attitude of openness to alternative viewpoints and opinions.

It can also help if partners make the commitment together and help each other stay focused on the task. Remember we're all in this together. If each of us gets better, we both win.

What are the payoffs for transcending the need to be right? The payoffs are many, but primarily, we become partners again. Our "identity" as part of a functional and loving couple nurtures each of us. Instead of a death struggle to determine who is right, who is "better" or "smarter" or "one-up," who has the correct view about the nature of reality, we can relax our commitment to any particular conclusion, and actually do some research together and seek out the most useful information. We can try to avoid minimizing and discounting the other and seek to explore the feelings and needs that underlie their passionate positions. And then make decisions based on mutual understanding. Or agree to disagree, or make an arbitrary decision, or take turns going with each other's opinion. "OK, let's try the bluefish with marinara sauce, this time, and we'll grill it the next time."

The Value of "Should"

Knowing ourselves also encompasses an understanding of the parental and religious and social injunctions that we have absorbed in the course of our lives: The *shoulds*.

We enter a marriage with a full cupboard of *shoulds* that we have collected throughout our lives. We *should* let ladies go first; we *should* keep a clean house; we *should* "neither a borrower nor a lender be"; we *should* spend quality time with the kids; and so on.

If we marry someone who more-or-less shares our cultural, ethnic, and socio-economic background, we might find that our *shoulds* line up better than if we come from very different worlds. This congruence in our perceptions of the *shoulds* can help immeasurably in the smooth functioning of the relationship. We run into trouble when partners' *shoulds* bump into each other.

> *Anita: It's trash night. I got it all collected, you should take it out.*
>
> *Tony: Why should I take it out. I always take it out. Maybe you should take it out. We should share that kind of stupid job.*
>
> *Anita: Oh, yeah? Well then maybe you should put Ryan to bed for a change.*
>
> *Tony: Why? He goes to bed better with you. You should do it. Besides, I should do the taxes tonight.*
>
> *Anita: You're impossible!*
>
> *Tony: No, You're impossible!*

Shoulds represent a persistent personal reflection of justice, and our knowledge of right and wrong; they represent our understanding of the order of things; our view of "if everyone did what they should, then everyone would be happy."

Should always implies some source of authority. So that, often, the first words uttered after someone tells someone else what he or she should do, are, "Who says?" The lame response is often, "I says," (because I have more power, or authority, or intelligence or experience). And if that doesn't cause a fight, it can make us laugh.

"In other words, I should do this because you say I should?"
"You got it."
(War or laughter on both sides ensues.)

Sometimes there is an invocation of authority: the Bible says, or the doctor says or Miss Manners says...

We begin our lives with parents who fill us with *shoulds*. And well they *should*. It's a parent's job to teach us the values of the culture and to instill in us a sense of right or wrong as defined by that culture. After all, a shared sense of values, of right and wrong, define a culture and enable its members to interact in a cohesive and functional way.

One of the problems with living in our time and place is that there are very few values about which we, as a culture in flux, do not feel ambivalent and conflicted, and about which we can all agree.

Old standby values such as cleanliness, wealth, even kindness, and generosity, have complex implications that often lead to controversy within intimate relationships.

"Honey, we should give $100 to the Heart Association this year."
"Not this year. We should really take care of Rachel's braces first."

In Chapter 9 we will see how competing values often cause conflict in relationships.

But there are other implications of the word "should" that create conflict for couples. Social psychology researchers, decades ago, discovered that some of us are more *authoritarian* in our personality styles than others. The more authoritarian of us tend to feel more comfortable when there are clear rules emanating from clear sources of authority. It helps us to know what to do, and when to do it. It helps us maintain order in a chaotic universe. "The Bible says," "Scientists say," "the sign says," "our accountant says," "the doctor says...." Others of us have a much looser and more flexible response to the voices of authority. We're more comfortable, even in the face of uncertainty, vagueness, and chaos; we tend to trust our own reactions, logic, impulses, and personal compasses. Of course, both courses can lead to wonderfully successful outcomes or terrible disaster, and an artful marriage, not to mention a successful life, often requires some wise balancing of these two approaches. Many of the fights that embroil couples involve the differing tendencies to follow authority or follow an instinct. These can turn into arguments where the transcript will reveal the utterance of a lot of "shoulds."

> *"Honey, the financial advisor said we should put money in the Hamburger fund."*
> *"No way, we should hide our money in the mattress. The economy is going to tank."*

Making and Keeping Deals

> *I didn't marry you because you were perfect. I didn't even marry you because I loved you. I married you because you gave me a promise. That promise made up for your faults. And the promise I gave you made up for mine. Two imperfect people got married and it was the promise that made the marriage. And when our children were growing up, it wasn't a house that protected them; and it wasn't our love that protected them -- it was that promise.*
> –Thornton Wilder, The Skin of Our Teeth

Some of the deals are explicit and some are understood, or at least we think they are understood until there is a conflict.

> *"I thought we were meeting at Starbucks at 7:00. Where are you?"*
> *"I'm at the one on Broadway and 79th. Near your office. Where are you?"*
> *"Oh, I thought you always went to the one on 76th. I'll walk back up there."*

Happens all the time. We make assumptions that don't match the assumptions made by our partner. Our assumptions usually stem from a lifetime of experiences. Our partners also have a lifetime of experiences and it's inevitable that our experiences will be different. Sometimes our assumptions will overlap, but often they won't. It's no one's fault, although it's usually tempting to blame the other guy. Simple miscommunications cause disappointment and frustration, sometimes anger, but they rarely kill relationships. If we care about growing our relationship we will be more careful about making the assumptions explicit next time,.

Here's another, more problematic, scenario:

"I'll meet you at 7:00 am, ok?"
"Sure."
Next day:
"Where were you?"
"Oh, man. I was so hung over that I couldn't even move until 11:00."

This kind of irresponsibility in keeping a deal is much more significant. This person's actions reveal a set of troubling, underlying problems, any one of which can spell disaster for a relationship. Perhaps this person values his/her partner so little that the partner's time (feelings, money, effort, convenience) doesn't matter very much. This attitude does not auger well for a successful relationship. On the other hand, the *guilty party* may have a real problem (in this case alcohol), which truly renders him/her incapable of being in control of his/her behavior. Such a person is deserving of our compassion, but it's hard to make deals with them. Anyone who continues to make deals with such a person after being burned a number of times has his or her own problems. A deal presupposes the *ability* of both parties to follow through.

This deal-keeping ability is a significant factor in maintaining any relationship. You wouldn't maintain a relationship with a plumber or auto mechanic who couldn't keep deals. This is not to say that we don't all screw up from time to time, and a heartfelt apology should usually be accepted. But we have to mean it, and be capable of convincingly communicating to our partner our true remorse at breaking the deal and of hurting or disappointing them. We have to make sincere efforts to rectify our behavior so that the same problems are unlikely to happen again. This ability to communicate our love and caring about our partner's feelings is a most important factor in virtually every interaction.

Don had issues with organization. He just couldn't seem to put his things away, even though he promised his wife, Tina, over and over again, that he would do it. She became exasperated and stopped trusting his promises and his apologies until Don enrolled in a Clear the Clutter course, dedicating time and money to the task. Tina appreciated Don's commitment.

Most wedding vows represent a deal, the kind of deal that Thornton Wilder so eloquently characterizes in the quote at the beginning of this section. Whatever the wording, we are usually committing ourselves to some pretty fundamental *actions* (not *feelings*, which we usually can't control). Love, cherish, honor, be true. If we follow through, we go a long way to getting on to the small pile of happy marriages. Marital Artists understand and embrace the *value* of keeping deals, and make every effort to grow in character so that they can follow through on deals.

Negotiation

Negotiations in a marriage, ideally, represent an effort to resolve conflict in such a way that essential feelings of love and respect are maintained and carried into the future. This is not always easy. A negotiation is a complex interpersonal event, but it is even more complicated in a good marriage. In such a marriage, not only do we want to feel good about the deal, not only do we want our partner to feel good about the deal, but we would also like both of us to feel good about the process.

A very successful salesman once told me that it is not enough to make the sale. He felt that it was important that his customer left the transaction satisfied that he had been heard, that his needs had been met, and that he had gotten a fair deal. The salesman was also committed to his customer's satisfaction after the deal. That way he was assured of loyalty, repeat business, and referrals. He saw every sales transaction as part of a long-term relationship. Conversely:

David once bought a video recording machine from a very slick salesman at an appliance showroom. The man convinced David that it was the best technology for the best price. After the purchase, David discovered that the machine was already outdated when he bought it and felt ripped off. When he went back to the salesman, he was told that he should have done more research, and basically, "tough noogies."

Obviously David felt embarrassed, and did learn a lesson about his role as a consumer. But he also felt ripped off and angry. Needless to say, he never went back to that appliance store. For the next twenty years in that community, David spent thousands of dollars on electronics, a refrigerator, a stove and other high ticket items but not a penny went to the dealer who manipulated and tricked him. That salesman made the sale but lost the relationship.

When we negotiate, even when we negotiate heatedly, as in an argument, we never want to lose track of the essential fact that: this other person is my love. We have a vested interest, as always, in ensuring that this other person, our best friend and love, concludes the negotiation with feelings of love and respect intact. For the Marital Artist, with very few exceptions, this relationship goal transcends any particular outcome that could possibly be achieved from the original negotiation. There are many potential obstacles in achieving this end.

Let's look briefly at our pesky inner child (we'll discuss more about this in Chapter 8). This inner child inhabits our being at our core, and sits ready to insert him/herself in all of our life's interactions. No matter how old, mature, or wise we get, our inner child, with all of his/her old manipulative strategies for getting what s/he wants; our inner child who is oblivious to the needs of others; our inner child, who developed skewed assumptions and limited understandings (or misunderstandings) long ago in our families of origin and in the sandboxes of days gone by, stands ready to project him- or herself into our daily interactions. When this happens in a marital negotiation, we cease to be concerned about our partner or the integrity of the relationship.

The Marital Artist understands that seeking to become aware of, and control, this inner child and getting to our more transcendent, adult self is the required first step in any successful negotiation with our spouse. It allows us to bring him/her into the frame; to recognize him/her as significant and cherished in the upcoming negotiation; to maintain a commitment to his/her satisfaction with the outcome and the process.

Unfortunately, negotiations for marital partners are often exercises in manipulation that leave one or both partners feeling enraged, abandoned, and lonely. The idea that, "We are two lovers, in this together," is cast aside early, if it ever existed, and is replaced by a bare knuckles, winner-take-all street brawl between desperate, adversarial inner children. A happy marriage will not last long once you recognize that you are married to the enemy. If you begin to perceive that this other guy is out to get you, to win using any trick in the book; the warm, cozy, safe sense of loving partnership will evaporate quicker than the morning dew.

Manipulation

Manipulative strategies can be identified in a limited number of forms, with infinite variety in their manifestations. Here's a partial list: bullying (yelling, threatening, abusive language or physical abuse), bribing, seducing, lying, withdrawing (or withdrawing love), pouting, nagging, ganging up (requires help of others). These manipulative strategies are often leftovers from childhood, when we learned how to get what we wanted quickly (or observed these effective strategies manifested by other kids or our caretakers). We might have been victims of these strategies ourselves and were unconsciously impressed by their power and effectiveness. Childhood is a time when we have very little real power. We also have very little tolerance for delay of gratification; all we care about is what we are able to get for ourselves *now*! It is a time when long-term relationships are either ignored, considered impossible, or taken for granted. Manipulative strategies tend to work in the short term. We can shut people up; we can make them disregard their legitimate rights and self-interests; we can make them more concerned about *our* needs than their own. But there is a cost. Every time a conflict is "won" by manipulation, an entry is made in the victim's unconscious or conscious ledger of injustice. This contributes to an erosion of trust and of belief in our partner's love. Over time we humans do not tolerate injustice well. Resentments build. Anger mounts until it erupts in a pattern of chronic squabbling; escalating patterns of manipulation and counter-manipulation; contempt; withdrawal; and emotional distance; psychological symptoms; and eventually revolution or dissolution of the relationship.

The Marital Artist, understanding the power and perseverance of the inner child, seeks to identify his/her own impulses to manipulate the outcome of a disagreement, understanding that wherever there is contention, there may well be such an impulse. At such times the Marital Artist strives to substitute a more cooperative and mutually beneficial strategy for the manipulative impulse. It doesn't always work. When they find themselves behaving manipulatively despite their best intentions, they stop it as soon as they can, apologize, and move on.

Art is not a thing; it is a way.
—Elbert Hubbard

Chapter 7 The Process of Marriage

The gardener discovers tranquility once she knows that the garden will never be completed. Only then will she surrender peacefully to the joys of gardening and begin to appreciate each, seed, bud, stem, leaf, and bloom.
–Chi Shing Chen

Jack Sprat could eat no fat, his wife could eat no lean. And so between the both of them they licked the platter clean.
–Nursery Rhyme

Every artistic effort involves a process. We begin with some unformed raw material: an alphabet, a tightly stretched canvas, a shapeless lump of wet clay, an untuned instrument, a scrap of metal, some wood, stone, fabric, wire, pigment, dye, or wool. These are all objects or materials pregnant with possibilities, waiting to be transformed into art by a process. We start with something basic and we use our imaginations our feelings, our intelligence, our knowledge of what others have done before us. We are driven by a fantasy, a hope, a vague sense of what is beautiful or playful or transcendent or inspiring or profound. We create something and then we create something else. We keep creating. We keep applying a process to the elemental things around us. We must, because we are artists, and artists create.

Many artists approach new challenges with a sense of openness and adventure. Some are willing to forego certainty of the outcome in order to surrender themselves to a process that promises to produce authentic art that flows from their hearts, souls and minds. In marriage, the embrace of a shared process is essential, because regardless of the "vision" of each Marital Artist, the "work" has to reflect them both. Unless we are willing to simply "fight it out" as adversaries, we must come up with a way to transform our individual quests into a collaborative adventure.

In marriage, it is not possible to completely abandon the focus on outcome. We do have specific shared goals in a marriage. We need a place to live, we need to eat, we need to bring up the children. But how we do these things is infinitely variable. As in any of the other arts, each individual Marital Artist may have a very clear image of what he or she wants the final work to look or sound or feel like. But in the essentially collaborative Marital Art (more like dance partners or band members than like solo painters or writers), the partners must find a way of transforming their individual visions into a shared vision.

The essential processes of marriage are reflected in much of the advice we get. Spouses do get a lot of advice. We're told that we should communicate more; that we should be more loving; that we should be patient and forgiving; that we should stand up for ourselves; that we should have high self-esteem and be respectful of each other; that we should be grown-ups; that we should be generous; that we should not sweat the small stuff; and that we should take nourishment and comfort for our souls from a broth derived from the carcasses of dead chickens.

All of these things are, no doubt, true. After all, some very smart people have shared them. I would like to offer another suggestion, and that is that we keep this in mind: a marriage is not a "thing," but rather, it is a "process," a sequence of transactions or a shared course of action, designed to achieve certain results. This process encompasses the things partners do, the ways they *act* in order to get from one place to the other, from one decision to the next, from one emotional state to a different one, from a state of chaos to a state of stability, from *me* to *us*. We benefit from an understanding that a marriage is always changing, and the ways that we participate in that change will, to a very large extent, determine the quality of the marriage.

Intention

I am going to sit in the shade with my beloved and eat lichees.
–Chi Shing Chen

There are many ways to "fall into" a marriage. We can be caught up in the passions of love and lust, feel pressure from family, friends, and biological clocks. Most of the time that's

125

how it goes. We're not all *that* conscious when we tie the knot. It's often only when we start bumping into the complex difficulties of life with another person that we start to think, "What are we really doing here?" Or, "this is not the way I imagined it to be," or, "s/he is not the person I thought s/he was."

At this point, or at any point along the way, partners can become intentional about their relationship. An intention reflects consciousness and a set of values and expectations. It articulates a promise to oneself to head in a particular direction. When two partners in a relationship share values and expectations and commit to heading in a mutually agreeable direction, life becomes more harmonious, fluid, and simple. When partners share their intention to interact fairly, lovingly, and respectfully, it contributes to a process that inspires trust and elevates souls. It begins to feel like the partners are rowing in the same direction, as opposed to steaming into each other with battering rams mounted on the bow. When the relationship gets stuck, there is something to refer back to. "This is not what we really intended to do. Let's get ourselves back on course."

Process and Intention

For many of us, perceiving our relationship as a process, itself requires an intention, as in, "I intend to consider our relationship a process." Why does this even require intention? It does because (in all areas of our life) if we do not intend to behave in a certain way, then we default into actions that may not reflect our highest aspirations for ourselves and our relationships. If we do not intend to see our relationship, our marriage, as a process, then we tend to see it as a thing ("my marriage") or as a state of being ("I am married"). A "thing" is passive and can only be changed by means of outside intervention, as by means of aging or entropy or some other external event (an affair, an illness, a bankruptcy, a child, a divorce). A "state of being" can be transitory ("I am no longer married"), and transmutable ("our marriage was bad but now it's good"). But our role in determining these states is generally perceived as passive.

I find it useful to view the relationship as a process, which is organic and fluid, which has cycles and transitions, periods of flow and periods of impasse, and in which the partners play an *active* role in its shaping. A process requires continual engagement. I think that partners who acknowledge this process and engage it actively have a better chance of adapting and coping with the inevitable impermanence of stable times whether good or bad.

When Snow White and Prince Charming went on to live happily ever after, what did they actually do? That is, what did they *do* to live happily ever after? If you take the view that they entered some marriage "thing," then you don't have to worry about it. They were in love; they entered a "marriage" (kind of like getting on a modern cruise trip, where everything is taken care of) where all the other details are incidental ("How much should we tip the steward, honey?"). But those of us who accept this view of marriage become disillusioned when we discover that the cruise is really a life long round-the-world, all-weather sailing adventure and transoceanic survival challenge undertaken with a crew of two.

To negotiate such an enterprise requires flexibility and adaptability as well as preparation, and an understanding that the process requires an openness and readiness for change. Just as a sailboat crew must be prepared when beautiful, balmy seas turn rough, marital partners must be prepared for the days when "lovey, dovey" turns into frustration and anger.

Marital Artists choose to view their relationships in this manner because it allows them to expect the unexpected, and frees them from the disappointment that comes when unrealistic expectations of "happily ever after" are inevitably frustrated. Viewing marriage as a process helps them develop skills and construct strategies for handling the inevitable impasses.

Before David married Susan they each believed that they had discussed most of the important issues that they expected to confront: things like children, religion, where they would live, and career plans. They entered the marriage believing that they shared a clear view of their future together. They quickly ran into a conflict of routines and they were surprised at how unable each was to accept the style of the other. David began to wind down his day at eight o'clock and whatever chores remained could wait until the next day. He had no problem going to bed with the sink full of dishes, and this attitude made Susan crazy. Before living with David, she had always felt a need to "tidy up and make the house nice" before settling down for the night. As petty as this may seem, the couple thought that this issue would drive them apart. They argued about it almost every night, because David's "down time" was very important to him, and Susan's "tidying up" was very important to her. It became a battle of control over who could make the other accept fundamental boundaries, which seemed mutually exclusive. Learning to reframe this "incompatibility" as a resolvable impasse made it possible for them to use a creative problem solving approach, revisit their personal preferences, and resolve the conflict. In this case, it wasn't that difficult. David came to understand that Susan experienced the disorder in an almost physically uncomfortable way, and Susan, likewise, came to understand that David had to shut things down at a certain point so that he could regroup for the next day. They decided to start dinner a little earlier and David agreed to postpone his shut down time by a half-hour. The big lessons, for them, were in understanding that they were different people with different sensibilities, wants and needs, that they cared deeply about each other's well-being, that they both counted, and that their relationship could

be viewed as a process. They came to see that com-
patibility and harmony are inevitably disrupted and
that impasses can be approached creatively. These
insights contributed to a feeling of confidence in
their relationship and in their ability to resolve the
impasses that will inevitably confront them in the
future.

For some reason our goal-oriented culture does not condition us to think in terms of process. Many of us have been taught to study for the test, run for the goal-line, work for the paycheck, complete the task, finish what you start, eat everything on your plate, find the pot of gold at the end of the rainbow.

Marital Artists understand that if they can appreciate the rainbow with their partners, the pot of gold can turn up anywhere.

So, like a forgotten fire, a childhood can always flare up again within us.
—Gaston Bachelard

Chapter 8 Stressing and Regressing: Visits from the Child Within

Deep beneath the crusty bark of the ancient oak tree lies the ring of its first season and, on top of that, the rings of all of the seasons that have followed.
–Chi Shing Chen

What's past is prologue.
–William Shakespeare

Marriage is our last, best chance to grow up.
–Joseph Barth

One of the great challenges of relationship is managing the expression of our "inner child." We need to discover a way to cherish and give expression to the wonder, joy, and spontaneity of our creative inner child, while developing control over the destructive, undisciplined, self-centered, and manipulative inner child.

There has been much written about the "inner child." For our purposes, we can think of the inner child as that part of ourselves that, historically, was formed in the "early seasons" of our actual childhood. It operates on the principles of child logic, maintains a child's behavioral repertoire, has a

133

child's unconscious expectations, and has the emotional needs and vulnerabilities of a child. The inner child is free of the constraints of adulthood, and so, often, is self-centered, curious, playful, spontaneous, mercurial, enthralled, creative, demanding, superstitious, impulse-driven, full of wonder, optimistic, lacking in frustration tolerance and needy for instant gratification. A very contradictory list of qualities. The inner child doesn't care about consistency.

There are many precious, wonderful qualities of the inner child that we hope to never lose. Some of us embrace this inner child; some of us indulge and pamper it; some of us are powerless against it; some of us fear and repress it. But it is always a force to contend with. We cannot live without it even if we find it reprehensible, troublesome, frightening, and inconvenient. And most of us wouldn't want to. Our inner child can be charming, and life without it would be dull and boring, running by efficient routine and guided solely by the demands of adult logic, responsibility, and duty. There would be no fun, no gumption, no spirit, no ambition, no wonder, no spontaneity, no creativity, no silliness, and no playfulness. No love. A Vulcan universe.

On the other hand.... as it has been observed before, if two people want to travel together for a long time they can't let their inner children drive the van. There needs to be an adult driving, or the van will wind up in the lake. Marriage is about deals, carefully and fairly crafted and children aren't always good at "careful" or "fair." The inner child is often willing to use any means at its disposal, fair or unfair, to accomplish its ends.

I will not discuss here the healing needs of the "wounded child," as these issues have been addressed by other writers, such as John Brazelton and Eric Berne. For our purposes, I am more interested in the "adaptive" inner child, the one that gets us what we (think we) need. This adaptive inner child will not be ignored or pushed aside. It is our last (and all too often our first) defense against annihilation and defeat. The adaptive inner child fights with everything it has to prevent losing that which it perceives is essential to survival. It's not always correct in its assessment, but so what? When the adaptive inner child takes over there's often no adult around to insist on reasonableness or a fair fight. We can try to remember that as children, we were relatively powerless, yet we had to develop strategies to help us meet our needs, especially our emotional and interpersonal needs; our attachment needs. We did this within the context of our first significant relationships. It was here that we learned our most fundamental lessons about how to attach to others. We'll talk more about attachment later.

Our inner child usually *demands* recognition. Neither we, nor anybody else can avoid the need to come to terms with our inner child, even if we try. It jumps in our face and yells, "What about me?" "Look at me," "Give me mine," "Don't do it your way, do it *my* way," "Clean it up *now*," "I want that," and so on. In a marriage the inner child manifests in many ways. Judith Viorst, in *Grown Up Marriage*, speaks of the "sibling rivalry" that is often apparent in marital competitions over attention, recognition, and even love. So many marital fights come down to competitions to see who can get the other person to *act* like a mommy or daddy while we adopt a child-like posture reflecting our need for attention, indulgence, forgiveness, care-taking, or some other form of nurturance.

Many of our so-called "adult" choices represent compromises with the demands of our inner child. For example, we work hard so that we can get the "toys" we want (the cars, the home theaters, the vacation retreats), the recognition, the revenge, the sense of security. It's not easy to acknowledge that these are needs of our inner child. We can rationalize all of these wants as perfectly grown-up and reasonable. ("I need some new jewelry because I need to start looking a little more professional at work.")

In our mature relationships we struggle to maintain a balance between our adult roles, values, and responsibilities and the demands of our inner child; demands for safety and security, pleasure, love, admiration, physical affection, and comfort. I, and many other therapists, have observed that most of the really destructive, ongoing fights experienced in relationships are actually fights between the most needy parts of two inner children. When stressed or needy, we may regress into styles of interaction that were formed and reinforced repeatedly in our earliest years. Like a non-native speaker, we often revert to our first behavioral language under stress. This "regression" leads to the "kitchen sink" arguments wherein we use any tactic in our repertoire so that we can be validated, get our way, or have our "rightness" established. Such behaviors are not attenuated by adult values of fair play, empathy, or compromise. They place us on an emotional ground that is primitive but feels familiar, and, though usually ineffective in achieving our "higher" marital goals like mature love, trust, and compromise, they sometimes actually "win" in the short run.

Scene opens on two children in a sandbox. They each want the same really awesome red dump truck.

First Child: Gimme that. I want it.

Second Child: No. I had it first.

First Child: You're a poo poo head.

Second Child: No I'm not. You're a pee pee face.

First Child: No I'm not. (First Child hits Second Child.)

Second Child: He hit me.

First Child: Did not.

Second Child: Did too.

First Child: Did not.

Second Child: Did too. Waaaahhh.

We're all capable of this kind of regressive infantile behavior in one form or another, especially when we're stressed; and when the perceived stakes are high. These tendencies reveal that we spend most of our lives living as eggs: fragile, barely formed babies on the inside with a thin shell of maturity on the outside. The Marital Artist is constantly working to transcend this regressive proclivity. Part of the work of Marital Artists is to develop awareness of the wants of our inner child, and create balance between the most negative aspects of the inner child, and the positive aspects of the playful and creative inner child.

Stress and Regression

Chronic stress is very destructive to relationships, because it tends to keep us in a needy, regressed state of being. It tends to keep our fragile inner baby curled up tensely behind the curtain, ready to explode, whining and flailing, into the next interaction, when exposed by the smallest ruffling breeze.

One of the great challenges of participation in any relationship is remaining a grownup under pressure. This is true because most of the really dysfunctional problems that couples have are sandbox wars. If our inner children aren't getting what they want, especially when personal resources are depleted, they'll do what children do in order to get it. That want may be anything from a toy (new car, computer, trip, dress, necklace) to a hug, to financial, emotional, sexual, or physical security, to being "right," to getting attention, to avoiding blame or responsibility, to being comfortable, to going to sleep. If there is a winner in a battle between inner children, there is also a loser, and that is never good for the long-term well-being of a relationship. To the extent that we can transcend the inner child, while maintaining awareness of his or her needs, we can find a way to get those needs met appropriately. We can try to respond to our partners as unique individuals, while still acknowledging our own needs, and thus seek solutions that acknowledge both of us all the time. As "adults" we can hold on to some higher goals (like the health of the relationship) even as our "inner children" maintain their single-minded infantile pursuits. When we are both highly stressed and in baby mode we're in trouble. At these times, there's no grown up to pull us apart, bring the milk and cookies, and make everything okay. Sometimes, in the short term, even one person maintaining a grownup perspective is enough to keep things from going too wrong. But, we must keep in mind that if that grownup is always the same partner (and the other partner consistently functions like a child), this will not provide a solution for the long term.

When we regress, often the inner unconscious wish is for the nurturing hand of the good mommy or daddy to take control and relieve our suffering: "There, there, sweetheart, put your feet up and relax. Mommy (daddy) will take care of everything." This "good parent" fantasy is as old as childhood and its manifestation in the conscious or unconscious wish for kindness, understanding, and nurturance will never end. If, in our actual childhood, we had a great mommy or daddy, then we hope to replicate their accurate empathy, warmth, thoughtfulness, self-sacrifice, generosity, and concern for our comfort and well-being. If we had rotten, or simply inadequate, parents, then we make up, in our minds, the good parents that we *wished* we had. This "fantasy good parent" presents its own set of potential problems, simply because it is not based on a real model and may reflect unrealistic expectations. Sorting out our expectations about nurturance can be another one of the ongoing challenges in a marriage.

We mature, rational, competent grown-ups may not like to admit that we still want a "good mommy or daddy." However, when we meet a potential spouse, we often behave as though we understand the dynamic perfectly by making unconscious offerings to the other person's inner child. We show them and they show us how much we can care, how well we can take care, how kind, thoughtful, and loving we can be. It's easy to get the impression that this wonderful person we just met will always be there for us. What we *don't* see, is the needy, childish part of this new and magical lover. Not yet. But trust me. It's in there. Sometimes we *do* see the needy child in the other person, and the child in us believes that we can get the love *we* always wanted by taking care of that needy child. That child will be so grateful for *our* love that they will surely return the love to *us*.

I know what you're thinking. Something like, "Ick! I don't do that. I'd never want that. Ick! Ick!"

There, there. It's okay. We all do it. We're all babies right below the surface. I know, you don't want to think about that. But it's really not so bad. Once you accept it, and *only* once you accept it, can you begin to get to work on the new project of transcendence. R. Buckminster Fuller described a state of human evolution that is like a chick emerging from the egg. The chick, having exhausted all of the nutrients provided for it inside the egg, pecks at the shell until it breaks through and then it is forced to seek sustenance in a whole new fashion. Marital partners often behave like that chick. Our old life, the life created out of our inherited proclivities and our reactively formed interpersonal strategies, sustains us for as long as it can, and then we crash into the shell. We feel stuck in old dysfunctional patterns and either shrivel up from the lack of new nutritional resources, or we break through to a quest for survival in a more inclusive and synergistic interpersonal environment. At that point we are ready to recreate ourselves as Marital Artists.

Where does our inner child hide when we are so responsibly leading executive committee meetings, or planning wholesome lunches for our three children? The truth is that even when we are behaving in our most mature and responsible manner, the *child* is always there, sucking her/his thumb and ready to explode on to the scene.

Inside all of us the ages of our life stack up like geological strata in the earth's crust. If you are 40 you also contain layers of 39 and 38 and 4 and 3 and 6 months, and these layers can emerge surprisingly unbidden and appear on the surface like an outcropping of granite that pushes through the surface of a pasture during an earthquake,

Given the right circumstances, any one of us can regress to an earlier stage of psychosocial development. Often, the stimulus is a stressor. With no more provocation than a poorly timed red light, a highly functioning company CEO can become an infant, yelling, hitting the steering wheel, and calling the light some adult equivalent of poo poo head. The whole thing gets easier if we can acknowledge it and even laugh at it.

Some of us find it difficult to embrace our inner child. (Of course, some of us also have difficulty embracing our "inner adult.") We're too fragile, too defensive, too insecure about the dangers represented by not acting as though we are adults, always in control. Ironically, it is our frightened inner child who feels the need to hold on to the absurd myth that we are always adults, always in control. The paradox is that those who are most secure and mature are the most capable of accepting both the joys and the vulnerabilities of the inner child.

When I grow up I want to be a little boy.
–Joseph Heller

Our inner child developed during our actual, chronological childhood. It developed organically as the qualities of our being – our physical, neurological, biochemical organism – confronted our very specific world, and developed an unconscious neuro-psychological survival strategy. We had to somehow use and adapt our inherited tools to come to terms with a world of adult personalities and other biophysical, psychosocial realities. We developed strategies unconsciously, and even transformed our neurological and biochemical-electrical structures early on, in order to match our germinating being to the demands of this powerful and often unreciprocating environment. If we were lucky, we developed means of coping and surviving in a variable world

142

where we had virtually no real power except that bestowed upon us by our caretakers working in conjunction with our inherited capacity to adapt. The strategies we developed may have included the ability to please others, or to depend on ourselves; or we found that aggression works, or humor, or charm, or passivity. We developed our cuteness or our intellectual gifts, we withdrew or attacked when angry, or we gave up, feeling powerless, hopeless, and depressed. More and more, theorists and researchers are discovering that some of the ways that we interact in our adult relationships had their origins in the persistent relational styles of our original caregivers.

These "attachment orientations" are rooted in early experience and are reflected in the relative ease or difficulty experienced in intimate relationships later in life. For example, researcher Barbara Kuerer Gangi, summarizing the literature on attachment, describes three attachment orientations.

Members of the first group were lucky enough to have had parenting capable of providing an appropriate buffer between their child's emerging physical and emotional capabilities and the demands of their world. The children of these parents are well integrated and able to evaluate early and later relationships realistically, "without feeling a need to distort them by dismissing them on the one hand, or over-idealizing them on the other." Such individuals tend to form attachments in adult relationships that are realistic and secure, with an acceptance of flaws, and an appreciation of virtues. For instance,

Thomas knew that his father had his "issues," but also appreciated his strengths. He was a little narcissistic and unaware that he was almost always the hero of his stories and he was often critical of some aspect of almost everyone else he met. He didn't "rip people apart," and his observations were never vicious and were often humorous. Thomas was also aware that if the other person had real troubles, his father was always extremely sympathetic and as helpful as he could be. He was able to appreciate that his father was completely devoted to him, was surprisingly non-judgmental about his actions, and usually provided a good ear and sound advice when Thomas came to him with a need. He was also a great cook, had many friends and was a great dancer. Thomas also was able to chuckle and shake his head about his father's skill at gently manipulating his mother in order to get what he wanted. Thomas' adult friendships and his choice of spouse were solid and mutually gratifying. He chose people in his life who had a good sense of themselves and he was able to see them in a balanced way, accepting both their strengths and weaknesses.

Some children must interact with parents who have greater difficulty maintaining emotional balance in their parent-child relationships. According to Kuerer Gangi, parents who are "brusque, functional, critical and rejecting" are over regulating of both the parent's and child's emotions and tend to discourage both the recognition and expression of feelings in both themselves and their children. They tend to be emotionally unavailable, unwilling or incapable of putting their own needs aside, or are inaccurate in reading their child's need. Children of such parents often learn to expect little in the way of support or nurturance. They appear extremely self-reliant, tend to either over-idealize or denigrate their parents, and minimize the impact of their early experiences on the development of their self.

Mary's mother was a successful businesswoman who managed a small company and was often on the road. When she was home she spent a good deal of time on the phone, writing, or arguing with Mary's equally busy father or the help about management of the household. Mary feared and respected her mother's reasonable, rational, competent way of handling every problem. She tried to please her mother by achieving success in sports, music, and school. Her mother praised her successes but had little patience for Mary's personal struggles, frustrations, and failures. Some version of "just deal with it" was her mother's typical response. Mary's mother rarely expressed any physical affection or comforting, empathic words. Mary became pretty tough and successful herself, and dismissed her mother's absence of nurturant behavior as "necessary," and claimed it provided good "lessons in life." Mary married an equally responsible, efficient, suc-

cessful, and emotionally distant man. Their childless marriage provided all of the material things that they could have wanted, but after a few years their "independent," parallel lifestyles led them both into affairs, and ultimately a very "grown-up" divorce. Mary's stoic response was that "these things happen."

Eddy was a "tough guy." He was a weight lifter with a shaved head, an earring, and arms covered in tattoos. He worked as a counselor with "bad" adolescent boys. "I never have any trouble with them," he boasted. "I treat them respectfully, but I keep my distance. They always know that I mean business, and they don't test me." Eddy's wife was angry and frustrated by his drinking, his emotional distance, and the way that he terrorized his children into obedience by yelling and withdrawing love, though he was never physically abusive. Eddy's defense was that he put a roof over the kids' head, kept them well fed, paid for their dance, music, and sports programs, and gave them "a hell of a lot more than I ever had." Eddy's father had been a "tough guy" too. "He used to beat my ass, sometimes with belts or sticks. But I usually had it coming. I was a wild kid." Eddy hadn't spoken to his father in over 3 years. They became estranged when Eddy's father neglected to come for a Christmas visit after Eddy had invited him. When Eddy was asked if he would mind *if his children cut him off when they got older he said, "I don't care. If they want to cut me off that's their business. I know I'm doing the best job I can right now. That's all I can do." When asked if he would like to develop a better relationship with his kids, he said, "don't get me wrong. My kids love me. They run to greet me every day when I come home from work. I just want them to grow up right, and I don't accept any nonsense."*

Some children must contend with other inadequate forms of parental nurturance. Kuerer Gangi describes a third type of attachment orientation that is characterized by "intense, clingy, emotionally reactive, often victimized relationships, fearful of abandonment." She links this type of adult relationship to a kind of parenting style marked by inconsistency. These parents can wobble between sensitivity, intrusiveness, and neglectfulness. They are unreliable. They are not skilled in "regulating either their own or their children's [emotional lives]." The child growing up in this type of household seeks emotional enmeshment and is often frustrated when their partner has different expectations. They are often in the position of needing reassurance or feedback about where they stand.

Celeste's mother was an alcoholic who vacillated between extremely attentive and affectionate overindulgence, and moody withdrawal and rage. Celeste worked evenings and could not tolerate the anxiety of being away from her husband, Sam, without calling him two or three times a night. Sam tolerated this attention for a while but eventually it got tiring, Sam felt smothered and became more and more irritated until he demanded that they seek counseling.

Abuse and Neglect

The developmental story gets much more complicated and difficult when our inner child suffered severe emotional injury through significant abuse or neglect during the formative early years. When this happens, the inner child, if s/he is lucky, develops powerful coping mechanisms that allow him or her to survive under these extraordinarily stressful circumstances. These coping and survival strategies become reflexive and unconscious, and they are often brought forward into future significant relationships. Unfortunately, the skills that enable survival under extreme negative conditions are not usually the skills that enable our highest expression in potentially functional relationships, or allow the blossoming of our transcendent selves. Fortunately, most of us unlucky enough to have experienced non-nurturing, or even abusive, childhoods, can find opportunities to grow beyond them and develop a transcendent relationship with regard to that negative past. The ghosts and demons of an abusive or traumatic past often last a lifetime, but with focus and energy and the utilization of available help, I have seen them managed and even transformed.

The Inner Child Should Not Be Driving the Van

The Marital Artist acknowledges and accepts his/her inner child. S/he works to develop a strong executive adult ego, which can allow the inner child free reign under safe and appropriate circumstances, but can place the inner child under control when an adult is needed to handle the demands of problem solving with a beloved partner. The discipline required to pursue the transcendent state of Marital Art is the work of an adult, although the inner child shares fully in the contentment and happiness that results. The transcendent state of Marital Art provides an integration of our childish yearnings and our adult strivings.

Sandy looked at the pile of bills and the mess in the kitchen and her stomach tightened. Her inner child could not tolerate the disorder and the fears that were triggered when she felt that the order of her life was unraveling. She was in the midst of piling dirty dishes into the dishwasher and mumbling to herself about the "pigsty" she was living in.

Dave was in the living room where he saw his 16-year-old daughter lying on the couch watching TV and texting a friend while she had a pile of unfinished homework on the floor next to her. His stomach tightened. He marched into the kitchen to begin a rant to his wife, demanding that she get "her daughter" into line. His inner child was very fearful that if they didn't stay on top of her, his daughter would "turn out to be a bottom-feeding dumpster-diver," even though there was a lot of evidence that she was a great kid, sociable, talented in a variety of ways and even moderately successful as a student.

"Don't you think you could spend a few minutes talking to your daughter? She's in the living room wasting her time. She's got a paper due tomorrow and a test on Tuesday."

"Can't you see that I'm trying to clean up the mess that the two of you made? I'm really sick of it."

"That can wait."

"Oh, really? Well, why don't you just do these dishes and I'll go kick the little princess in the butt because you don't want her to think you're a meanie."

"I'm on her case plenty. I just don't want to be the bad guy all the time."

At that point both Dave and Sandy realized what they were doing and they began to playfully exaggerate the child-like quality of their argument.

(Whiny voice) "Well you're a scaredy-cat-wimp-face. Afraid of your little girl. Whaaaa, whaaaa."

(Same whiny voice) "Oh yeah, well you're afraid that the neat-police are going to walk in and give you a slob ticket. Boo, hoo."

They both started laughing and hugged each other.

"Tell you what, why don't you do the dishes, and I'll talk to Sara. Thanks."

This, however, is the sublime melancholy of our lot that every You *must become an* It *in our world.*
—*Martin Buber*

Chapter 9 Attitudes and Values

We have very little time. Let's sit together and watch the stars.
–Chi Shing Chen

Fundamental values color every action that we take. Marital Artists make choices continually in their relationships, and it is inevitable that these choices are shaped by attitudes and values. Furthermore, these attitudes and values inform the *manner* by which we satisfy our needs. At any given time, we choose our course of action from among all that are possible. Either our attitudes and values guide us or we are left to *react* out of reflex, or habit, or old, unexamined learning. And choices made reactively often do not reflect the Marital Artist's highest strivings.

What are values anyway, and how do they affect a marriage? Values can be reflected in our thoughts as beliefs about what we deem most important in our lives, or they can be reflected in our behavior as actions. Both of these aspects of "values" affect our marriages, but probably our actions are more relevant. "Actions speak louder than words," goes the old cliché, and for good reason. We're not talking about

153

what's true or false here, or what is right or wrong. Values are about what is important to *us*. Sounds simple but actually, it's more complicated than that in practice because most of the time we have values that are in conflict with one another. Here's an example:

> *A poor but honest man with no health insurance discovered that his wife had an illness that could be cured only by a particular medicine that the man could not afford, and time was of the essence. He sneaked into a pharmacy and stole the medicine.*

This story obviously pits the value of honesty against the value of sustaining life. The man chose his wife's life, and although this is, perhaps, an overly dramatic example, we are often confronted by our own, personal, conflicting values.

> *Thomas knew that his wife, Danielle, was looking forward to a day at the beach with Thomas, the kids, and her sister's family. Thomas knew that he would enjoy the outing, and what's more, he valued "family time" and making Danielle happy. Unfortunately, he also was expected to finish a work project by Monday, which he would never get done if he did not invest the whole weekend. His values of achievement and job performance were in conflict with the value of family time.*

> *Elaine wanted the house to be spotless and organized when her son's tutor came over for a lesson. She was all set to get to work on the messy house when*

her old college friend called and said she was in town for a brief stopover between flights. Elaine could not clean up and also visit her friend. She truly believed that presenting a dirty house to a visitor was disrespectful, but she also believed in the importance of nurturing and respecting friendships.

Ian had put aside a day to repair a leaky ceiling that had the potential to cause real damage to his walls and floor. When his wife called to ask him to attend a neighborhood meeting about a critical local political issue, he was torn between his values of attending to his property and being a good community member.

We all have to struggle with these kinds of internal or "*intra*-personal" value conflicts all the time. They make us scratch our heads and force us to decide which of our choices represents our more salient value. Often, however, the values of marital partners come into conflict with one another, as well. These "*inter*-personal" value conflicts also require sorting out and require some kind of resolution, which can take a variety of forms from discussion to all-out ongoing war. Values that can be at odds in instances of marital discord may be things like: Planning vs. Spontaneity; Strict Authoritative Discipline vs. Dialog and Negotiation; Conservative choices vs. Exciting choices; Spending vs. Saving.

Marital Artists see a creative challenge in the task of working out value and attitude conflicts. However they also understand the need to start with a shared sense of the *fundamental* values that shape the processes of their marriage, among these being *trust, respect, and counting each other all the time.* These specific values are essential foundations of the Marital Arts and of a productive and transcendent process.

Among the values that help us make art out of our relationships, probably the most fundamental is the recognition of our partner as a unique and valuable person who counts all the time. This is a value; an ideal, which in practice is not so easy to attain. Our inner children don't give a hoot about our values (or our partner's needs and wants either, for that matter).

When Martin Buber talked about "You" and "It" he was describing a profound distinction that we can easily lose track of in our everyday experience. When "You" become an "It" to someone else, it means your essential humanity is diminished. The other person sees you solely as a means to his or her ends. Unfortunately we do this all the time, not only to the people we interact with casually, but also to the people we profess to love the most. We can easily forget the essential humanity of our customers, our sales people, our clients, our teachers and students, police officers, politicians, doctors, lawyers, or anyone else from whom we need something to proceed with our lives. These people sometimes collude in the obfuscation of their essential "personhood" by assuming a role.

In the case of marital partners, this tendency to not see the "You" results from my need to experience your "qualities" in terms of how they reflect on *me* or serve *me* in my life. I have chosen you, we might say, as an "object" because you are beautiful, handsome, rich smart, funny, generous, talented, or a good cook. I may have selected you for these qualities because they enhance *my* life. But what about "You"? You probably experience your life as something quite different and more inclusive of your full experience. How can I love *"You"* if you lose the qualities that I have sought in you because they serve *me*? How do I transform you from an "It," an object that serves my needs, into a "You" whose essential being I value for yourself?

In order to do this I must be able to separate myself from my needs; to transcend them, if you will. As hard as it might be, we can aspire to a state of being wherein *we are not our needs*. This is confusing and difficult. We all have needs. But in order to relate to you as a "You," in Buber's terms, I must be able to experience "You" as a unique and separate being, and not simply as a means to my ends. And here's another wrinkle: If I treat you solely as an instrument to my ends, the relationship must necessarily diminish you and sooner or later you will resent it. Finally, and ironically, to the extent that you are not a "person" to me in your own right, I will eventually come to have contempt for you because at my center, I want a relationship with a *person* rather than with an instrument, however useful.

Choosing to relate to a *You* as opposed to deriving benefits from an *It* in our relationships really makes a difference in the everyday experience of our partnership. It behooves us to get clear about our relationship values. We must ask the question: "What represents the greater value, choices that serve short term personal gain, often at the expense of our beloved's interests, or choices that serve *You* and *Me* and the entity that is *"Us"?*

We have to be careful to understand that by making choices that serve the collective *us*, we are not making martyrs of ourselves. We are not discounting our own needs but choosing to see our needs as part of the needs of the larger entity that is *us*. We are choosing to value a *process* that seeks to incorporate the wants and needs of both partners *all the time*. This value decision rests on the assumption that by enhancing the well-being of the couple, the individual partners will thrive. If you don't share this belief, then what's the point of being committed to one another?

In their book, *The New Couple*, Maurice Taylor and Seana McGee are really talking about new values. Traditional marital values served specific outcomes of marriage: economic security, maintaining a home, raising the children. These authors suggest that for a modern couple to be successful in their relationship, they must develop different values. These new "Laws of Love," as they call them, include values of "love of self," "mission in life," and "emotional intimacy." Other values include maintaining "chemistry," "weeding out unhealthy preoccupations," "establishing emotional integrity and safety," "deep listening," "equality and respect," "peacemaking," and "transformational education." The authors have described a set of skills, which represent a set of instrumental values. They call this set of instrumental values "emotional literacy," which includes "deep listening," "anger management," "conflict resolution," and "negotiation."

This orientation goes very much against the current of our modern way of life. We are geared to think in terms of personal goals, of self-advocacy, of getting our share, however, to be a Marital Artist is to maintain the value of the partnership most of the time.

What comes from the heart, goes to the heart.

—*Samuel Taylor Coleridge*

Chapter 10 Communication

The quest to discover the heart of the beloved is as a journey through a great maze. You will be dizzy and lost often. It is easier to find your way when you ask for directions and then listen carefully.
–Chi Shing Chen

What we have here, is failure to communicate.
–Captain, from the film Cool Hand Luke

Communication is one of the incredible gifts that we humans were given by the Gods or nature. Communication permits us to turn the processes that are internal, hidden, and private, into processes that are external, open, and shared. Marital partners don't have to let the laws of entropy rot the canvasses and crumble the foundations of the beautiful art that we are creating or turn our music into noise. We don't have to drift apart simply because we find ourselves floating in different directions like model boats on a breezy lake. We can let each other know where we are going and what we are thinking and feeling. We can talk, and argue, and make deals and take each other along on our journeys. Effective communication represents power in a marriage and can contribute to the processes that make marriage work.

The power embodied in effective communication enables us to share our personal inner worlds, and when we do this mindfully and creatively, it can produce Marital Art. Conversely, when we communicate ineffectively, or worse, manipulatively, we can create confusion, resentment, and distrust, and undermine the foundations of our relationship.

Couples who are experiencing marital difficulties are often eager to attribute their difficulties to communication problems. The nature of these communication problems is usually somewhat harder for partners to articulate. They have vague complaints such as, "He doesn't listen to me," or "She goes on and on, and I lose my patience." I find that the so-called "communication problem" often reflects much more substantive psychological and interpersonal issues such as those discussed elsewhere in this book. For example, John Gray, in *Men Are from Mars, Women Are from Venus*, talks about the different ways that men hear the complaints that women express, and why they sometimes respond defensively. As an example, Gray points out that a woman may say, "We are always in a hurry," and the man hears it as the criticism: "You are such an irresponsible man." The man's likelihood of hearing the statement as criticism may be directly related to his level of stress, low self-esteem, general psychological vulnerability, or specific experience in his family of origin or with this particular woman. It may not be *just* a communication issue. As mentioned in another section of this book, we are more likely to act from our inner child, in a defensive or aggressive manner, when we are psychologically vulnerable.

However, sometimes "communication issues" are really communication issues. The processes of communication have been studied meticulously and new discoveries continue to be made.

So what do partners mean when they complain that they cannot communicate, especially when they tell you that they communicated well during the early days of their relationship? This communication thing is really very vexing.

We are not the only species on earth that communicates. Animals communicate their desire to mate (yoo hoo, I'm over here), to signal danger (let's get out of here), pain (ouch, stop it), hunger (give me some of that), the location of food and water (over here guys), tenderness and connectedness (let me help you get those bugs out of your fur).

We humans communicate for many of the same reasons, but, in addition to all of the standard primate-type messages that we exchange all the time with every other human we encounter, there are special communication challenges for people – and especially for couples.

You Cannot Not Communicate

The anthropologist Gregory Bateson pointed out that you cannot "not communicate." We are always communicating even when we are still and quiet. We may be communicating our desire to be left alone, or to not be noticed. We may be communicating our melancholy or our anger. We may be performing the role of "rock," in the first-grade school play. A person who remains still and quiet may be communicating his desire not to interact.

There may be other more mystical dimensions to communication. Some have speculated that we communicate pheromones, or even "vibes" when we are out of sight or at a distance or even when we are dead. There have been recent discoveries of "mirror neurons" that allow us to react, at primitive neuro-biological levels, to the behaviors of other people, in order to feel deep empathy.

The Marital Artist understands that the more you are aware that you are always communicating, the more you can take responsibility for *what* you are communicating, and to whom.

Different Channels

One of the truly confounding aspects of communication is that we communicate many things in many ways at once. Sometimes one level of communication contradicts another, or the messages coming through the different channels don't support each other. For instance, sometimes our words conflict with our para-communications – our body language or voice inflections or even choice of vocabulary. This is significant because we communicate nonverbally more than we think we do. Communications researcher Albert Mehrabian has famously suggested that in our efforts to understand the feelings and attitudes associated with a communication, we are 55% dependent on facial expression, 38% dependent on tone, and only 7% dependent on words.

Two or more of our communication channels can support, compliment, or contradict one another. For example, Mora says she's tired and asks Tom to turn off the light, but she smiles and winks as she says it. She may not really be saying that she's tired!

Tanya wanted Robert to spend the evening with her. She had a vision of the two of them cuddled on the couch with a glass of wine and a bowl of popcorn watching a romantic movie. Robert announced that there was a game at the Convention Center and that his buddy had gotten tickets. He asked Tanya if she minded if he went. "Do whatever you want," she said curtly, her jaw clenched as she tossed the newspaper onto the floor. Robert read her body language and called his pal back to tell him that it might be a good idea if they went to a game on another night.

We look for congruence in our communications with others. That is, we most trust messages when the context, the body language, the voice inflection, the vocabulary, and the message content are aligned.

John was engrossed in a TV movie when his wife walked in and asked whether he would be willing to drive an hour to look at a house she was interested in. Without looking up, he mumbled, "What? Huh? Oh, yeah, sure." She thought, "Maybe I should ask

*him again later. Analyzing the context made her re-
alize that she really couldn't trust his response as a
true reflection of his feelings.*

How Do I Feel About You?

Every time we initiate a communication there are at least
two layers to the message. The first layer involves our surface
message, the content of our message, for example, "Please
pass the salt." If these words are read on the page they are
interpersonally neutral (that's why emoticons were created
to clarify the emotional tone of a texted or emailed message).
But when this message is presented in person, there is a secondary layer that is at least as important as the first, *and it is
always present*, even when communicating with strangers.
The second layer of the message contains information about
how I feel about you. I can have a loving tone and a glint in
my eye, a musical ring to my voice that makes the phrase
sound like a love song. I can be formal and polite, indicating
that I want to show you respect and maintain some appropriate distance. Or, I can be short and impatient, as though
I've asked you for the salt twelve times already and you are
the most annoyingly inattentive person in the world. I can
ask for the salt in a distracted way that implies that I barely
notice you and that you don't count very much to me right
now, or I can scream my request, indicating that I am very
angry at you.

You cannot avoid this second layer of communication no
matter what you do. Whether you are gurgling at your new

baby or asking for an oil change from your mechanic, you are always communicating how you feel about the other person. It is one of the reasons that we often walk away from an encounter with someone, regardless of the superficiality of the interaction, with a positive or negative feeling.

It is useful to be aware of this fact when we communicate with our partners. We like to know where we stand with our lover and feel reassured when we get the message, "You're wonderful"; or "I'm loving you." When we get the message, "You're annoying"; or "I have contempt for you"; or "You make me ill and if it weren't for the children I'd be out of here as fast as a sneeze," it creates tension and sets up, or reinforces a dynamic of conflict, disharmony, and defensiveness.

This tension helps to explain why the silent treatment can be such an effective and painful manipulation. It creates uncertainty in the status of the relationship, and this uncertainty creates anxiety. "Please talk to me. Are you angry about something? Did I do something wrong? Is there anything I can do to make you forgive me? Do you still love me? Are you leaving me?" This type of communication lets the other person know that he or she stands outside the relationship. "We are not together," it says, "and if you want to be together again, you'd better do what I want." This is not a comfortable message for someone who wants the status to be "together."

The regular use of endearments such as "dear" or "sweetheart" has traditionally communicated togetherness.

"Please pass the salt, honey," includes a statement about my feelings toward my partner.

Marital Artists make an effort to sustain a sense of security in their relationship by communicating the loving nature of their bond through word, gesture, and deed.

Three Kinds of Communication

Let's discuss three kinds of marital communication challenges: First, and always, we must communicate in order to know where we stand with each other. "Are we close or distant?" "Do you love me?" "Are you angry at me?" "Is my status in any kind of danger?" "Do you want to get naked?" "Are you *still* angry at me?"

Second, we must know what our partner is thinking, feeling, what our significant histories have been, our hopes and fears, our plans for the future. This requires a form of communication we can call *sharing*.

Third, we try to influence each other, so that our partnership can provide for our needs and wants. Let's call this type of communication *politics*.

Where Do I Stand?

This is communication at its most primitive level. We want to know whether we are in or out, connected or not. The nature of this type of communication changes over the course of the relationship. Upon first meeting, partners may signal that they want to get closer, or they may signal their ambivalence about getting together. This stage is expressed in the dance of closeness and pulling away that occurs in many early courtships. As feelings intensify, the stakes get higher and anxieties often increase for one or both partners. There might be an increased frequency of fights and making up, expressions of jealousy, and a need for reassurances. The breakups and reconnections are all an attempt to clarify the level of connectedness and commitment, the boundaries and expectations that will shape the relationship. The most meaningful aspects of communication at this stage are nonverbal (probably the most meaningful aspects of communication at *all* stages are nonverbal). We look to the other person's body language, voice inflection, touch, attention, subtle, often subconscious behavioral synchronies (eye contact, body orientation, matching postures, eye-blink and breathing rates, skin flushing, grooming behaviors). And though I know of no research to support this, I suspect that the more consistent and congruent these para-communications had been in family of origin communication, the more likely that communications will be read accurately in subsequent relationships.

This need to know where we stand is a large part of the early maneuverings of a potential relationship. It has to be, because the relationship's future is uncertain at this stage. At this point the emotional investments are still small and one or both of the potential partners can decide that they want out, so they must constantly jockey around the question of how much to give in order to minimize risk of hurt and disappointment while at the same time maximizing the option to continue to move forward. There's a kind of emotional, "You go first," "No, after you," "No, I insist," quality to this phase of the relationship.

For many couples, for a variety of reasons, this is as far as they get. They are stuck in a yo-yo limbo of on-again, off-again, pursue and withdraw, commit and quit and re-commit, that can go on for a lifetime, without ever arriving at a stable, secure stage of trusted, unambivalent commitment. Often this inability to either stay in or get out is rooted in early, unresolved attachment issues.

How do we signal that we are a "we"? Sports teams do it, most obviously, by sharing a name, a uniform, and a home field. More subtly, teams and groups develop their own, shared sense of history, linguistic and behavioral signifiers, jargon that is theirs alone, and a shared sense of humor (in-jokes). They speak in terms of "we" when they could also use the term "I."

"You pitched a great game today, Sammy."
"Well, we made some great plays in the field. and we got the hits when we needed them."

Marital Artists demonstrate their sense of "we"-ness through a variety of verbal and nonverbal means as well as through their inclusive process, which emphasizes their commitment to ensuring that both partners count all the time.

Ann: "Ed, Carol is on the phone. They want us to come over on Friday night."

(Ed starts to shake his head and gives hand signals that indicate, "no way.")

(Ann speaks into the phone): "I'll have to get back to you, Carol. I think we might have something else going on."

As commitments fall into place, the need to know where we stand in no way diminishes. It's just that if we're lucky, and we and our partners have fairly minimal scarring from our childhoods and previous relationships, and if we have done a good job of communicating the message "You are loved and safe and secure with me," the urgency for constant attention to this status question may settle into the background, although it always requires regular maintenance. Some of us, for a variety of personal reasons, can never get to a place where we can effectively communicate consistent love and emotional security to our partners, just as some of us, for similar personal reasons, can never accept that we are loved and safe.

If you truly aspire to be a Marital Artist, you must explore the demons that prevent you from giving or accepting the message, "You are loved."

On the other hand, if we are feeling distant or disconnected at any particular time, and this happens in the best of relationships, Marital Artists can address the status question with very direct and clear communication.

First Partner: "I'm feeling disconnected, honey. I'd like to feel close. What can we do to get close?"

Second Partner: (Taking first partner's lead)(Pick one or more or make one up) "Let's cuddle up and watch a movie." "Let's go up to bed." "Let's take a walk." "Let's light some candles and read poetry." "Let's jump around on the trampoline." "Let's feed each other cookies." "I want you to apologize for yesterday," "Let's give each other foot massages." "Let's play backgammon." "Let's _____ (fill in the blank)."

Sharing

A second type of communication that serves us in all aspects of our relationship is a style that we can call *sharing*.

Do you recall how you communicated shortly after you met and fell in love? Most of the communication was of the sharing style. This style of communication requires nothing of partners other than that they cherish what each other is saying. You are not trying to get your partner to *do* anything. You let them know your favorite foods and colors and movies; you tell them about your family and your summer vacations as a kid. You do not ask them to take out the garbage, or get a better job, or change their hairstyle, or wear sexier clothes, or stop tracking mud into the house. This sharing style of communicating builds closeness. At some deep and primitive level of our psyches we want to be known and to be loved for who we are. This style of communication is part of the magic of the infatuation stage of new relationships. It is supported by and consistent with the hidden biochemical transformation of our bodies that is happening simultaneously.

Sharing involves the sometimes not-so-simple effort to have our partner understand us, to know us, to have access to our inner life. Sharing is essential in the early phases of a relationship in that it serves to define, support, and maintain the special status that we have with each other. Sharing keeps us connected as the relationship matures and confronts impasses. It helps us consider each other as distinct and highly regarded individuals as we make decisions and resolve conflicts. In more mature phases of the relationship, sharing represents one of the best strategies for maintaining closeness and preventing emotional alienation. Sharing also plays a role in the *political* style of communication that will be discussed below.

Since we are moving streams of passing sensations, feelings, memories, hopes, dreams, fears, thoughts, and imaginings, our sharing is like a dipper full of our awareness that we pass along to our partners as gifts. The more we share, the more our partner gets to know, and remain in touch with the shapes, patterns, and textures of our life.

Of course, sharing isn't always welcome or appreciated. Sometimes one partner experiences the flow of "sharing" from the other partner as intrusive or, perhaps, overly demanding of time and energy. The first partner describes many details of the day's experience such as who s/he saw, and spoke to, what they said, how their children are, their recent purchases, trips; or s/he talks about work, office politics, obsessive gripes, disappointments, conflicts. The emotional purpose of this kind of "chattering" does not always represent constructive sharing. Boundaries and limits must be respected. Remember that sharing needs to be, well, shared. Sometimes it serves some purpose for the sharer, but not the listener at a particular time because s/he is not in the mood, tired, preoccupied, or distracted. Or, conversely, sometimes one partner wants access to the other's heart and soul when that person is not in the mood, tired, preoccupied, or distracted. There must be a balance between one partner's need to share and the other partner's desire and ability to listen. A Marital Artist can gauge the availability of his or her partner at a given time and make accommodations while always remaining respectful of their partner's desire to share or ability to listen. Each partner must take responsibility for the level of his or her need to share, and ability to be receptive. As always, we both count all the time. We try to be available to our partners, while being aware of our own needs. The need to share must be balanced with a respect for the temporal and emotional boundaries of our partner. A sensitivity to time, place, and emotional mood go a long way in maintaining the balanced flow of communication, and are close to the essence of Marital Art.

Alex: Hey, I wanted to tell you what happened when I saw my brother today.

Taylor: Huh, oh, you know what honey, I really want to hear about it, but I feel like I have to finish unpacking while I'm in the mood or it won't get done. Give me ten minutes and I'm all yours.
Alex: Sure.
Taylor: Thanks. I'll be right there.

Some of us find it hard to share or to accept sharing. We feel chronically stressed or fatigued, and withdraw to take care of ourselves. Or, for some of us, there is a feeling that we have nothing to say. Maybe we fear that we have nothing to say *of interest* to our partner. We'd like to think that our partner cares about our inner lives, but maybe we don't trust that they do. This lack of trust can reflect experience with this partner, or it can be a holdover from earlier life experiences.

The process of sharing requires two things: first, that we are willing to make the choice, and expend the effort required to share, and second, that we trust that our partner will care about what we have to share. Sharing takes the form of communicating that which we are, were, or hope to be; what we imagine, believe, think, or fear; how we feel today physically; what we want for breakfast; how we feel about each other; stories of the day; a fright; a dream; a fight with a co-worker; and on and on. There really is no limit. And again, the purpose of these "sharing" communications is just that you will know what's going on with each other. When sharing, partners don't want anything except attention and caring. Sharing requires trust. It is difficult to pass this valued content of our life's experience to someone unless we trust that they will cherish it.

John Gray has pointed out that in Western cultures it seems that men have a harder time with sharing than women do. Women are brought up bonding with friends through verbal sharing. For men, early bonding experiences are often action-oriented and competitive, and sharing creates vulnerabilities that can be used against them. As boys jostle for status and power, they may become much more circumspect in their decisions to share. And for many men the impulse to share is inhibited completely. An 8-year-old boy might think twice before telling his buddies that he's afraid to climb a tree. He might expect this information to lead to teasing or loss of status unless his friends are an unusually evolved bunch. By 12 most boys have already learned how to inhibit the kind of sharing that will make them socially vulnerable. The common stereotype of men who are "strong and silent" is illustrated by the apocryphal story of the two old friends who sit in a fishing boat all day limiting their conversation to "hey, pass the worms." (As with most generalizations, there are many exceptions, men who are very comfortable with and skilled at sharing their inner world.) If there is any truth to the stereotype it is based in some complex mix of nature and nurture – that is, the way men are acculturated, and maybe also the way they are built.

Whatever the reasons, it is my experience that marriages benefit from communication that involves large portions of sharing. In this realm men might have to learn to trust and work on their sensitivities and insecurities regarding status and worth. Women would do well to be vigilant in their trustworthiness as listeners, and maintain awareness of the peculiar sensitivities that many men grow up with regarding criticism, judgment, and loss of status.

If we want to encourage honest sharing in our partners, we must listen openly and uncritically. We tend to do this naturally and unconsciously during the early stages of our relationships. It is one of the reasons that love blossoms. Later on, things change. Nothing will stifle sharing more quickly in a marriage than a judgment, or worse, turning the sharing into an adversarial battle. This occurs when the material shared does not meet our expectations, or it provokes feelings that are uncomfortable to us. At these times we have the option of checking the impulse to challenge, criticize, or react defensively. We must keep reminding ourselves that the real goal is maintaining an environment of safety, and in order to do this we may not always hear exactly what we want to hear.

> *Elena was feeling a warm romantic glow as she put down her book and saw Aaron sitting on the other side of the couch. She wanted to know that he was feeling the same way.*
>
> *"What are you thinking," she asked, in a tender voice.*
>
> *"Oh, nothing," he answered quickly.*
>
> *"Come on. Tell me," she continued, openly.*
>
> *"Oh, you wouldn't understand," he said.*

"Come on. I really want to know. Trust me." And she
really thought she did.
"OK. I was wondering who the Yankees were going
to play in center field this season," he said.
"You're a jerk," she said as she picked up her book.
Aaron scratched his head.

Politics

The third, and perhaps the most complicated, aspect of communication, an aspect that we can call *politics*, involves messages designed to get our partners to do the things that we want them to do. After all, we never cease needing or wanting to provide for ourselves as individuals and we often seek help from our partners. Our biological organism has needs all the time, as does our psychological self. Then, after we serve our needs we can get to the pile of wants, which, again, depending on our individual psychology, can range from nonexistent to infinite.

In the beginning, from the first moments we meet, there is always *some* element of politics. We do want *some* things (to be noticed, to be called), but primarily, the early stages of relating emphasize sharing. Later, as chemistry shifts and other relationship dynamics come into play, we start behaving more "politically." We begin to exert influence and introduce efforts to get our partner to do things that are good for *us*. We may have a certain hope for a particular kind of lifestyle, so we try to get the other person to help us get it; one person may want to live closer to his or her family so s/he asks his/her partner to move; we want the windows cleaned and we want our partner to do it; we get turned on by receiving flowers, so we ask our partner to change to suit us.

All of this maneuvering to achieve our personal agendas is conducted in the communication style of *"politics."* As in any political contest, the object is to get what we want, and of course, there are many ways to do this. In a marital relationship there are some ways that are better – ways that enhance the basic goals and health of the marriage – and ways that are worse – ways that undermine the basic integrity of the marriage. It is very important to understand how our political communication strategies contribute to the well-being or dysfunction of our marriage.

When we connect to another person, somewhere along the line, we define his or her role in our need- and want-satisfying strategies. We seem to be thinking, "well, I've gotten along okay up until this point in my life, but now that I've hooked up with this wonderful helper, it's as though I've got an extra pair of hands and eyes, a new pile of money, a second car and twice the energy to get things done the way *I* need them to be. Ain't it grand. (Oh yeah, of course I'll help him/her too)."

We've learned how to expect and accomplish need gratification (or not) from our families of origin and our original community of peers. We've learned to expect caring (or not), consistency (or not), competence (or not), respect (or not). We choose our partners, at least in part, based on our fantasized belief in their ability to meet our expectations (or hopes) and then we proceed to interact as though they share our same need gratification template. But of course our mates have different templates having come from different families, having different friends, different experiences, different physiology, and so on. This lack of template congruence creates no end of conflict as we go about the business of trying to get the other guy to do what we want (all of which seems perfectly reasonable to us).

How we go about the process of political communication enormously colors the quality of our relationship. If we lobby for our wants and needs fairly, and we maintain the Marital Artists' understanding that our partner counts all the time; if we can communicate love and respect even while we are disagreeing; if we remain responsible adults and don't succumb to childish, manipulative strategies; then our political communication will enhance our relationship rather than corrode it. But maintaining artistic political communication is a *huge* challenge, a challenge that represents one of the major obstacles in the quest for Marital Art. It is so easy to lose our focus and revert to the sandbox wars, where our inner children battle it out using any and all manipulative means at their disposal: We nag, we threaten, we pout, we call names, we yell, we withdraw, we take unilateral action, we disregard our partner's expressions of their legitimate wants.

The political communication process becomes even more complicated when we don't even know what we want. Often we're confused or ambivalent and our mixed messages to our partners reflect this chaotic state of our minds. Let's look at the nature of ambivalence.

Ambivalence

At the end of each day, Yes and No must find a way to share the bed. Certainty will not warm us on cold and lonely nights.
–Chi Shing Chen

Our culture values clarity of action. *When in doubt, do something.* Our need to assert this value represents a denial of our ambivalence or a willingness to simply ignore it. As Chi Shing Chen suggested, we often have mixed feelings about everything, and have to find a way to live with that fact, our "wish" for clarity or decisiveness notwithstanding. In the classic American film, *High Noon,* we sympathize with Marshall Kane's dilemma because of the nature of the ambivalence that lies beneath the surface of his heroic behavior. When he is abandoned by all of those who might stand to support him and he must make the decision to fight alone, we sense his fear and his desire to leave the situation as an unspoken counterpoint to the strong sense of responsibility to do the right thing. His wife, Amy, also has to struggle with her strong, Quaker belief in non-violence and her love and loyalty for her husband.

In these characters' powerfully heroic stances we experience the tension of the drama because we identify with the ambivalence that lies beneath the surface. Maybe we're not so sure that we could be as heroic as they are, even though we might understand the "right" thing to do. A hero performs heroically *despite* his or her contrary motivation to behave in a self-serving manner. We could even say that the definition of a hero is someone who experiences ambivalence and yet chooses the "right" course of action; the one that most reflects his/her highest value.

Marital partners are confronted by this kind of ambivalence over and over again. There is almost always an inner conflict, an ambivalence, about decisions that are made in the service of creating a balance in our lives. Ambivalences are those inner struggles that we experience as we make our own personal decisions in life, and they invariably affect our relationships; some of them more than others.

For instance, Diane may be ambivalent about changing the course of her career; giving up investment banking in order to open a candle shop. Such a decision may have important implications for her personal satisfaction, but it may also have important implications for the lifestyle of her family. There is ambivalence in the working out of this decision. A person may *really* want a new toy (car, boat, TV, piece of jewelry) and, at the same time, understand that the money spent could be used to purchase a trip that his/her partner would enjoy. S/he is confronted by ambivalent feelings.

Such ambivalent situations occur all the time in relationships and they must be resolved in *some* fashion: choose the one, choose the other, do nothing, create a compromise, agree to disagree, flip a coin. The resolution of these ambivalences represents a set of challenges close to the center of the

Marital Art. Marriage is comprised of two people whose ambivalences must undergo a process in order to fall into alignment and allow decisions to be made that do not leave a residue of resentment.

Once we are aware of our own tendencies to ambivalence, it is easy to understand that our partner also experiences ambivalence. Even when we are on different sides of the argument, it is possible to understand that we both have some ambivalence about most decisions. Identifying our ambivalences and sharing them allows us to be more creative in our efforts to find solutions. The less functional alternative is to polarize the ambivalence, usually unconsciously. This means that one person will take one side and the other person will take the other and they'll battle it out until one of them wins (and the other one goes away resentful!).

Acceptance of ambivalence helps us increase our levels of compassion for ourselves and for others. It helps us understand the difficulties that we all face getting through our days. Some of us find this process easier than others. For some of us the task of analyzing an ambivalent set of options is resolved quickly and there is little regret about "the road not taken." For others of us, the task of making decisions is excruciating.

In our relationships we often suffer from personal battles with ambivalence. So often we want to do the right thing for our partner and for the relationship, but we are reluctant to suppress impulses toward gratification of ourselves. We are often confronted with the unpleasantness of trading the best personal choice for the best relationship choice. It's not always easy, and requires a leap of faith for the Marital Artist: namely that we are trading short-term personal gratification for the potential long-term gratification of a healthy, happy, trusting, loving relationship. Sometimes it doesn't have to be so black and white, and solutions can be found that represent compromises between two extreme choices.

The Marital Artist stays with the dance, creating balanced steps that match the often paradoxical polyrhythms of their ambivalence. Solutions require the same qualities and skills that we keep needing over and over again in the practice of our Art: trust, self-awareness, effective communication with large portions of sharing, empathy, and an intention to engage in a loving process where we *both* remain aware that we *both* count, all the time.

The complexity of our ambivalences is often confusing to ourselves, and all the more so to our partners. We want to help out with the dishes but we're "really, really tired"; or we want to lose 10 pounds but the dessert looks especially good; or we want to have sex but we don't want the visiting in-laws to hear anything; and on and on. If I only share one half of my ambivalence, I am not giving a complete message. A complete message includes all our feelings, consistent or otherwise. Our culture, unfortunately, overvalues decisiveness and consistency. (When was the last time that you heard a politician articulate his or her uncertainty: "I'm really not sure whether the cement plant is a good idea for our community.") If we don't appear "decisive," we look "weak," or "wimpy"; we're labeled "waffler." Maybe some day our culture will again value careful deliberation and the thoughtful weighing of options, and ambivalence will be accepted as part of the human condition. Until then couples will have to go against the cultural grain and give each other permission to hold mixed feelings.

This is not to say that concrete decisions don't have to be made. They do. However, especially in our intimate communications, we should not be ashamed of the ambivalence underlying all decisions. Remember, courage often consists of making a decision even in the face of ambivalence. Sharing ambivalence allows us to have compassion for the decision maker and recognize the sacrifices that all decisions entail. We should avoid creating a marital communication culture that demands consistency and linearity. This is our most intimate relationship. It's a worthy goal to seek a level of trust in our relationship that gives us the freedom to express our confusion and ambivalence and trust our partner to help us sort it out.

Polarization

Sometimes in a political marital argument, each partner's ambivalence gets polarized in the form of rigid, adversarial positions. For instance, in the case of an expensive purchase, one person takes the role of "frugal, responsible steward of the family resources," while the other person takes the role of "fun-loving, generous stimulator of enjoyment and excitement." In reality both partners might feel both sets of feelings.

> *He: The new boat would be a blast, but can we afford it?*
> *She: The new boat would be a blast, but can we afford it?*

But because of the truncated nature of communication, and the need to appear consistent, we choose a side and argue it tenaciously, often becoming manipulative and attaching disparaging personality traits to the other person as a result of their entrenched position. "You're so stingy." "You're so irresponsible."

> *He: I'm sorry, but you're being really irresponsible. We can't afford a boat now and you know it.*
> *She: C'mon, you know we would love a new boat. It would be so cool. Isn't it beautiful? Don't be a cheapskate like your father.*

If both partners owned both sets of feelings, they might be able to make a decision without the acrimony that results from seeing the other as an adversary, from using negative, manipulative strategies, and from placing the other in a negative light. In such cases joint decision-making becomes a complex exercise in ambivalence resolution and is not simply a matter of who can yell louder or deliver the most stinging insults.

For the Marital Artist, it is useful to keep the larger relationship values in mind at all times. The question becomes,

"Is it more important to get the color sofa I want, or to have a functional, happy marriage? Do I want to 'win' this particular battle or make sure that my partner feels valued and cherished?" If we keep our eye on the relationship prize, then some of the other wants become less imperative. If our wants really are important to us, then it becomes essential that we lobby for them strongly, using all of our communication skills, including trust, sharing, and respectful, non-manipulative conflict resolution strategies.

The Challenge of Communicating in the State of Ambivalence

I tell my beloved that I must nap even though I would like nothing better than to walk with her in the meadow. She nods and smiles and says, "We'll go another time."
–Chi Shing Chen

Much of our marital political communication suffers from lack of clarity because we mishandle our ambivalence. To be clear in our *political* communication requires that we develop an ability to express all parts of our ambivalence.

When we are *sharing* with one another, there is usually a tolerance for uncertainty and ambiguity. We will usually demonstrate high levels of patience and support as our beloved tries to clarify his or her feelings, memories, hopes, and dreams. When it gets down to *marital politics,* however, our impulse is often to be less patient because we may have competing interests that compel us to resist our partner's efforts to get what he or she wants. In our more grownup moments we want our partner to get what he/she needs or desires because we are invested in his/her happiness. But we also want to get what *we* want. It is an easy slide to becoming adversarial, demanding, petulant, rigid, accusatory, angry, and defensive.

It is extremely helpful if we can continually be aware of what we want, *all* that we want including what is best for our partner, and for the relationship. Because of the multi-layered nature of the wants and needs being expressed, by two *different* individuals, marital political communication can be very complex, multidimensional, and inconsistent. The Marital Artist understands this complexity and seeks to address it in all communications.

> *"I need some space, and I also want you to know that I love you and I'm looking forward to being with you in a little while."*

> *"I want the new couch, and I also want you to know that I am considering your feelings about the family finances. Let's explore our options."*

> *"I want Johnny to have the new video-game, and I also respect your feelings about over-indulging him. Let's talk more about our parenting concerns."*

The heart of the challenge is to hold on to our commitments to care about our partner's concerns even in the face of our own wants. If we seek to be Marital Artists, we must resign ourselves to the fact that neither of us will get all that

188

we want all the time. In exchange for this acceptance, we gain an environment of trust and caring, which permeates every negotiation. We try our hardest to help our partners get big chunks of what they want. And, we trust that they are trying just as hard to help us get what we want.

Our "inner child," about whom we spoke in Chapter 8, is not that interested in acknowledging the ambivalence or in resolving it in a manner that considers our partner or the needs of the relationship. The inner child seeks the greatest level of immediate gratification and disregards long-term concerns, or the concerns of anyone else. Sometimes, in the face of confusion or ambivalence, our inner child even hopes that our partner understands us *better* than we understand ourselves, and can discern our meanings and clarify our wants even when our meanings and wants aren't clear to ourselves.

"Why didn't you just come in and hold me? I felt so awful."
"Uh, because you told me to go away?"
"Well, you should have known that I needed to be held, you jerk."

Even the language we use to express ourselves is influenced by our "inner child" and, specifically, the training we got in using the language of feeling when we want to share our wants with our partner. When we are brought up by competent parents, we often *are* capable of understanding and articulating our needs and feelings. We learn about the language of feeling when a parent or nurturant other helps us to label (some would say "construct") the meaning of our experience. For instance a child who is sitting alone, staring into space, may be feeling discomfort. Then mom comes over and says, "Are you feeling lonely, honey? I know that you must be sad that your friends can't come over." Mom was exactly right, or at least close enough to help junior put a label on his feelings. Now there is a linguistic signifier for a vague emotion, and the next time he feels it, he can label it and refer to it himself.

But a person who has never had the opportunity to learn, or to value, a vocabulary of feeling, and an appreciation of the complexities of multi-message communication is at a disadvantage in communicating with a partner, and would benefit from counseling that might help to remediate this deficiency.

The Marital Artist, always on the lookout for that naughty "inner child," understands that, especially in *political* communications, it is best if the "inner child" remains happily distracted, or napping, and the conversation takes place between our "inner adults."

Symbolism and the Currencies of Caring

Since we all grow up in different environments, different families, different communities, different peer groups, we often have different understandings of the meaning of symbols. Some symbols are fairly universally interpreted among a wide range of people: red means "stop"; green means "go."
190

Within a particular family, however, very idiosyncratic meanings can be applied to symbolic items, gestures, or even linguistic patterns. In Carol's house, when her narcissistic and controlling mother gave a compliment such as, "I like your hair," Carol came to understand it to mean, "I'm noticing your hair because I don't really like it very much." Consequently, Carol grew to be reflexively skeptical about compliments. When her husband, Dave, complimented her, she would often get defensive and self-conscious, and be unable to accept it in the spirit in which it was given. Dave became skittish about complimenting Carol.

Another, common, misinterpretation of symbols involves the ways that we communicate caring. In his book, *The 5 Love Languages: The Secret to Love that Lasts,* author Gary Chapman describes the ways that marital partners miscommunicate because they do not understand their partner's preferred language of love.

Steve would always spend part of Saturday morning checking out Beth's car. He would check the oil and tire pressure, the windshield wipers, and the brake fluid. He always maintained the yard and the outside of the house. He understood these actions as expressions of his love and caring for Beth. In the world he came from, that's what men did to express caring. Beth took care of many inside chores, but considered them just household chores. To express her caring for Steve, she would pick up little presents for him when she was out; a book, a CD or some

other little "thoughtful" gift. Steve was an "action"
guy, and didn't really read much or have a lot of
time for music. Secretly, Steve thought that the
"gifts," just cluttered up the place and wasted
money.

Beth became resentful that she was so "thoughtful
and caring," and Steve "couldn't care less." Both felt
misunderstood and taken for granted.

For Steve and Beth the symbols of their caring were neither understood nor appreciated. Marital Artists make an effort to reinterpret the behaviors of their partners from the other's frame of reference, and to convert their currencies of communication. They also share their perspectives and histories and personal meanings, so that their partners understand what their gestures mean to them. They make an effort to express their caring in currencies that their partners can appreciate. Finally, they make efforts to create new symbols over time that are meaningful to both partners.

The Role of Sharing in Marital Politics

The "sharing" and "political" styles of communicating are really fundamentally different. As previously stated, the goal of *sharing* is simply to have the other person understand our inner world; the goal of *politics* is to get the other person to alter his/her behavior. Politics represents acknowledgement of an unavoidable aspect of relating: we are different people, with different wants and needs, and we must have a means of lobbying for ourselves.

For Marital Artists there is an essential role for sharing in political conversations. Sharing, as much as possible, must be the style used by both partners to express the underlying emotion and the ambivalences that inform any political interaction. Sharing lets us express how important this particular want is for us and why. It lets us communicate our mixed feelings, and translate the yearnings of our "inner child." It turns a political conversation into an opportunity to reinforce the firm foundation of love, trust, and respect that supports the highest aspirations of the relationship.

This is not an easy task, and Marital Artists are always struggling against the demons that threaten to spin us off course into adversarial combat and childlike sandbox fights. Developing the focus and self-discipline to remain loving partners while engaged in political communication is one of the ongoing challenges of our lives.

For Marital Artists, the ideal is to engage in political communication that plays out fairly, with partners trying never to lose sight of the larger goals of the relationship: to ensure that both partners count, and that outcomes are sought that consider the needs of both individuals. In functional relationships, the political dynamics *include* sharing so that outcomes reflect a mutual concern for the feelings of each individual. In fact, among the constants in the pile of wants of each of the Marital Artists is the desire that their partner be happy. These couples understand that, "If you're not okay, then I'm not okay."

Anita: Honey, I'd really like to talk to you about your leaving dishes in the sink.

Rick: Uh, ok. What would you like to say about it? I just don't think it's that big a deal. I usually get to them eventually, and if I don't, nobody dies.

Anita: Dishes in the sink are like a red flag for me. They make me feel like my life is going out of control. It's probably old training, but I can't help it. It makes me feel very unsettled and makes my stomach tighten up. I know I'm a little compulsive about it, but I just can't relax until all the dishes are washed and put away. I know you usually get them done before you go to bed, and you do so many other things around here, but I like the kitchen clean before I sit down to relax. Do you think that you could do them right after dinner? Or would you like to trade some chores and I'll do the dishes after dinner?

Rick: Well, I like to just relax for a while right after dinner. But I don't mind doing the dishes and if it's that important to you I'll get the dishes done right after we eat.

Anita: Thanks, honey. I really appreciate it.

Manipulative Political Communication

In dysfunctional relationships, communication is heavily skewed toward a manipulative political style with the politics being adversarial, vicious, and unfair. It discounts or diminishes the other and erodes trust. It can create resentment, as well as vindictive payback or alienation. Our culture is full of win-lose transactions such as these; certainly the wars whose reports fill our front pages daily are designed to be win-lose contests (although they're often lose-lose), as are the gladiatorial events we call election politics. Sports are designed as win-lose competitions as are courtroom battles. Even business transactions are often win-lose engagements. We can put enormous energy into being "a winner," and, conversely, one of the worst things that can be said about someone in our culture is that they are "a loser."

Marital relationships are easily swept up in this cultural climate, and develop an almost reflexively adversarial posture. We are convinced that on this issue, or, in really dysfunctional marriages, on all issues, our partner is our enemy. S/he wants to deny me the things that I want and to which I feel entitled so that s/he can get what s/he wants. We must fight for the right "to go out with the guys," or to "take that ceramic course on Thursday evenings."

"You can't stop me. You're not my father (mother)."

"You're spending too much." "You are such a slob."

"Would you put out the light? YOU don't have to get up early, but I do!"

"She does not need a horse!"

If my inner child enters the discussion, and I lose focus on my commitment to my partner, then I might feel free to use whatever self-serving strategies I can come up with in order to win my point. Manipulations take a number of forms: I can demand, nag, yell, bring up old business, threaten, shout, guilt-trip, name-call, whine, pout, withdraw, withhold love, gang up with the support of a friend, or simply stonewall. I might win the point, but positive feeling in the relationship will inevitably be tarnished. Feelings of resentment can lead to retaliation or a response of anger, alienation, withdrawal, or abandonment of the marital project.

Manipulative political communication is often easy and reflexive, but it is the antithesis of Marital Art, and we should work hard to recognize it and find more relationship-enhancing alternatives. When manipulative communication strategies slip into the process, and they will, they should be labeled and eliminated and apologies should be offered. Then we can get back to the process of creating Marital Art.

Ask For What You Want

The politics of marital life can be simplified enormously if we simply know what we want and ask for it, and encourage our partner to do the same. As discussed above, we may not always get all of it, but if we ask, we stand the best chance of getting some, or even most of it. If our partner really doesn't want to give us what we want he or she can simply say "no." This, of course, works best if there is a pervasive atmosphere of trust that partners care deeply about

196

each other's happiness and well being. It also helps if partners employ the "Yes" rule, that is, we say "yes" to each other's requests unless there are compelling reasons not to.

Many couples go 'round and 'round, avoiding a direct "ask":

"What would you like for dinner tonight?"
"I dunno, what would you like?"

The speaker is leaving him/herself out of the equation. Instead they could have tried a statement of preference and a question:

"I'd like a big Caeser salad for dinner. What are you in the mood for?"
"I was hoping we could go out."

Now the cards are on the table and a discussion can help work out the differences. Not really that big a deal.

A bigger problem occurs when a partner expresses his or her want obliquely or manipulatively, transforming it into an attack on the other. One of the most common and non-productive examples of this is "describing the other's behavior". This almost invariably triggers a defensive reaction where a simple request might not.

"You always leave your shoes in the living room."
"No I don't."
"Yes you do."

As opposed to:

"Honey, I'd appreciate it if you'd put your shoes away."
"Okay."

Another example:

"You made me look like a fool at Sarah's the other night."
"Well, you shouldn't have taken the last piece of cake."
"I didn't."
"Yes you did."

Here's what it might sound like if the sentiment was phrased as a request:

"Would you please take me aside if you want to tell me something that might embarrass me in public?"
"Sure, sorry."

Sometimes it seems very difficult to formulate our thoughts into requests, especially if we don't feel we have the right to ask, or we've been taught that asking is greedy, or if we are angry, ashamed, or embarrassed; or if we are feeling distant from our partner. But asking directly is really the shortest distance between two points. It's worth practicing.

One More Thing

It is useful to keep in mind that often, despite our best efforts, we will still be misunderstood. All we can do is keep trying until we run out of time.

I know there is strength in the differences between us. I know there is comfort where we overlap.
—Ani DiFranco

Chapter 11 Coping with Life Together

Like children jumping into cool water on a hot summer day, we enter marriage in a hurry. Only then, if we are lucky, do we learn how to swim.
–Chi Shing Chen

A couple was camping in a beautiful mountain forest on their anniversary weekend. Evening was descending rapidly and they knew they had to hurry to get things put away before it got too dark to see. Suddenly, the husband saw a large shadow start to move at the periphery of their campsite.

"What's that?" he asked nervously.

"Oh my God! It's a huge bear," answered his wife, just as frightened.

"W..w..what should we do," stuttered the husband.

"Let's run for it," answered his wife, already running.

"We can't outrun a bear," shouted the husband after his wife.

Over her shoulder the wife answered back, "I just have to outrun you."

In Chapter 8 we described a desirable kind of stimulating, life enhancing stress called "eustress," the positive kind of stress that makes us feel alive, stimulated, and challenged. We also mentioned what happens when stress intensifies beyond an optimal point and devolves into "distress," a term we are all too familiar with. Distress starts to erode our ability to function and enjoy life, and at high levels leads to a complete breakdown of systems.

Our lives are stressful: children, jobs, difficult people, money, weather, pets, bodies that don't always behave the way we would like them to, household chores, computer crashes, car maintenance, in-laws, faulty products, sitting on "hold," traffic, trash, mail-in rebates. The list goes on.

As the stressors mount, we may begin to fantasize about a spouse who knows exactly how to fix it or make it all go away. We might think about how amazing it would be if every time we felt irritable or stressed our spouse knew, just *knew* exactly what to do without even having to be told. What a dream! When you want to be left alone, without distractions or interruptions, they leave you alone, and protect you from the intrusions of others. They keep the kids away and screen your telephone calls. When you want help with the cleaning up, they pitch right in. They do it just the way you would have done it without any prompting or reminding. And what about those weary times when you'd just like to be cuddled without any fear that it's going to turn sexual? Your partner understands this and gives you warm cuddles without any sexual expectations. And speaking of sex... your partner understands the stress-reducing power of hot, erotic sex, exactly the way you like it. No need for talk or time wasting foreplay. Wow, wouldn't that be great?

This person we're describing does sound very much like the good mommy or daddy of our dreams (minus the sex part, or course).... Okay, what's wrong with this picture? Maybe we didn't notice the entrance of *Inner Baby*, stage left. "You mean my spouse is not my good mommy or daddy? Whaaaaaaa. But I'm stressed. I *want* my good mommy or daddy." Wouldn't it be great if our partner was always able to be the good mommy or daddy of our dreams whose only wish is for our happiness? The selfless one who has infinite patience and strength and wisdom and self-control? The one who can make all of the bad feelings go away?

Yes, it would be nice, but there are some problems: First, and this might be obvious, *You did not marry your mommy or daddy*! Second, what if our spouse is stressed and needy at the same time that we are? What if they want *us* to be the good mommy or daddy at the same time that we want *them* to be the good mommy or daddy? Hmmm, then we have a situation. It can be seen in homes everywhere: we can refer to it as *throwing your partner to the bear*. Our stress or exhaustion levels are so high that we don't care what our spouse is suffering. We're no longer in this together. It's every person for him or herself. "Save yourself! It's a *bear!*"

These situations, where both partners are experiencing high levels of distress, and low levels of inner resilience, demand the most extreme efforts of self-control, strength of character, and heroism. In other words, Marital Artistry of the first order. It may be the single most powerful reason why most couples don't make it to the small pile of The Happy Ones. Good team-work and cohesion under pressure are among the virtues that lead to breathtaking perform-ances, such as Oscar-winning movies, Grammy-winning re-cordings, World Series and Super Bowl championships, vic-torious armies, and successful businesses. Oh, and great marriages.

Stress reduction, stress tolerance, stress management: these are terms that are thrown around a lot. We are stressed. We "advanced" moderns think we're such hot stuff: big houses, 2 cars, 3 kids in private schools, 52" flat screen home theaters, and 4 jobs between 2 people to support it. (Note: I don't know if it's true, but I once heard from an an-thropologist that many of our prehistoric forebears spent something like five hours per day in hunting and gathering and other work and the rest of the day was spent relaxing. The good life, right? Of course, those folks only lived to be 38 years old... It's always something.) Learning how to come to our relationships clear and full, taking responsibility for rea-sonable lifestyle choices, developing our own stress man-agement strategies, and avoiding infantile expectations of care-taking, can go a long way in easing the burdens of rela-tionship.

Part of the magic of the early stages of infatuation in our relationship comes from the fact that we don't yet expect that it is our partner's job to reduce our stress. We may not even want him or her to know that we are experiencing stress. Ironically, this would be at the time that our partner happens to be more than willing to share in all of our stress and help to soothe it away. It's a wonderful minuet of mutual nurturance that keeps us afloat in the love-bubble. Somehow, after the bubble bursts, many of us find ourselves dancing the Frantic Monkey all on our own.

Thresholds

Discomfort seeks relief. When we are too hot, we seek coolness; when we are hungry we seek food; when we are lonely we seek company; when we are uncertain we seek clarification. Much of our life is spent preventing stress, or pursuing relief from the feelings of physical or psychic discomfort. One of the frustrations of relationships is that we usually have different thresholds of discomfort and different styles of resolving our discomfort.

Some of us can take on huge loads without cracking. Others get overwhelmed by seemingly minimal loads. It makes sense. After all, some of us can run faster than others, lift more weight, hold our breath longer. Why shouldn't there be differences in our tolerances for work or stress? And in the face of these individual differences, how do we pursue our quest for fair sharing of the burdens of our life? As much as we may not like to admit it, we all keep our ledgers of justice, and when we feel we are carrying more of the load, we can easily begin to resent a partner who seems to be shirking his or her share.

Anez knew that Evan became frazzled easily when it came to paperwork and organizational tasks. After about 10 minutes doing bills or taxes he became irritated and exasperated. He would get up from the table and throw his hands in the air and storm from the room, muttering under his breath. He didn't want Anez to think he was just passing the buck to her, but he really felt like he would explode in those situations. She trusted him when he told her that, and told him she would do the paperwork if he would pick up some other chores. He said he would and followed through with his commitment.

In this case, in spite of the apparent threshold differences regarding tolerance of paperwork tasks, Anez was able to feel that there was an overall balance in the apportionment of all tasks because Evan picked up a greater load somewhere else.

What happens when the "ledgers of justice" just do not balance for one of the partners?

Danis was pretty laid back. Very little bothered her. In most areas of life she could easily "go-with-the-flow." The things that she did crave were attention and affection. Her husband, David, was very "sensitive." He was bothered by clutter, loud noises, cold temperatures, bills; he was "compulsive" about the car, the yard, the dog and the dry cleaning. At the end of his work day he was "exhausted." He had "no energy" to do evening chores and resented any plans that were made requiring him to leave his recliner, although from that perch he would often complain about the household's shabby state of affairs. He was successful at his work and made a good living for his family, but, unless he was on an extended vacation, free of stress, he was not good at "down time," playfulness, or affection.

Danis understood that David had very low thresholds in all of these areas, and believed that his frequent discomfort was real. But she became more and more resentful that she often had to adapt her lifestyle to meet David's needs and he seemed incapable of accommodating hers, minimal as they seemed to her. It didn't seem fair.

We experience different thresholds and appetites in most of the areas of married life. Karen might think the music is too loud when it's above a "3," while Kevin likes the pounding vibrations at level "8"; Ellen likes the temperature at a toasty 74, when Aaron starts to sweat at temperatures above 68; Thomas can't stand a single cup left on a counter, while Pat would barely notice a sink full of dishes for two or three days. Allison would like to go out on a "date" with her husband every weekend, while Bill feels it's too much even every other month; Jack would like sex twice a day if he could get it, while once a month is fine for Erin.

These differences in thresholds and appetites create discomfort at different times and for different reasons in people. If Karen says, "The music's too loud," she means, "The music is too loud for *me.*" It's really uncomfortable for *her.* When Kevin responds with, "No it isn't," what he really means is, "I like it like this; it's the way I enjoy myself." The real issue is about her "discomfort" versus his "enjoyment." Unfortunately, the "argument" usually takes the form of a debate on the "rightness" or "wrongness" of each person's position. It's as though there were some judge, who happens to be unavailable at the moment, who would determine how loud music was supposed to be, and that one of them was right and the other one was wrong.

The prosecution might bring in data about what "normal," or "nice," or "responsible," or "considerate" people do; the defense might appeal to an article that was recently in the paper; or someone might raise the objection that, "you could do this for me after all I do for you" (exhibit A: the ledger of justice). The fact is that in a lot of these "appetite" or "threshold" issues, there is no right or wrong, just "different." For some couples they are impossible to work out, while other couples seem to work them out almost effortlessly. The couples with difficulties frequently feel like adversaries; they each see the other person as trying to rip them off, or of being insensitive; they don't trust that their partner will act in a loving, generous way; they must be on guard, defensive, protect their turf. These postures may truly come from experience with *this* partner, or they may be legacies from past relationships or from childhood experiences in the family of origin. During times of conflict they seem to forget that "everybody counts." Sometimes these battles devolve into struggles for control, and the original appetite or threshold differences are forgotten. Resolving the differences with mutual love, respect, empathy, and consideration ceases to be the goal. It is replaced with a no-holds-barred effort to win.

Marital Artists strive to have a natural, easy flow in their give and take and are usually trusting and trustworthy in the relationship. They trust that the other person loves them and would not behave in a selfish manner, just as they are loving and trustworthy in their actions toward their partner. They act as though everybody counts all the time. This is not to say that working things out is always easy. But there is a different tone to the conflict resolution process. These partners do not speak to each other as though they were enemies. They maintain the ability, even when angry, or far apart on an issue, to communicate that they still love, respect, and care about each other. They fight fairly. They stick to the issue, without bringing in a garbage bag full of old, unresolved stuff. They do not demonstrate animosity or contempt. They don't manipulate. Also, and this may be most important of all, they are able to laugh at their differences no matter how contentious it gets.

This is a tall order and most of us will struggle with the achievement of this ideal. Behaving in the manner of a Marital Artist requires the transcendent posture of a centered, balanced adult. Yet we know that in times of stress, our behavior is often commandeered by our self-serving inner child. Remember that striving for Marital Artistry is an on-going process, and that we are all works in progress.

Karen: Kevin, that music is too loud for me.
Kevin: C'mon, honey, listen to that bass. Ya gotta feel it through your feet.
Karen: Please, it's hurting my ears.
Kevin: If you'll go upstairs just 'til I finish this CD, I'll put on the headphones for the rest of the night.
Karen: How about you wear the headphones for the rest of the week.
Kevin: Ouch. OK. You drive a hard bargain.

Managing Stress and Anxiety

In addition to differences in appetites and thresholds, partners have different personal styles of managing their anxiety. Anxiety is one of the mechanisms of regulating our personal lives or social interactions. It is that nebulous feeling of discomfort that lets us know that something is not right. We might feel it as a muscle tension, such as in our backs or necks, as a tightness in the stomach, as a feeling of restlessness or jitteriness, or as a nagging persistent thought. Whatever else it is, it is uncomfortable. When we experience it, we want it to go away.

After dinner, Roger sat down to start a new book. His day had been full of tension and he longed for this time to escape and regenerate. He couldn't think of doing anything else until he had some down time.

Margaret had just finished working in her office grading papers, and she came down to tell him that the house was a mess, that there was work to be done, and that she would appreciate his help. Roger felt like the long arm of stress was reaching into his cave and choking him. He snapped at Margaret that the dishes weren't going anywhere and that he'd clean up the living room later. Margaret silently fumed at Roger's childish irresponsibility and his sexist willingness to let her do the household chores even though they both worked all day at their full-time jobs. She was tired of the same merry-go-round playing out every night. She felt frustrated and abandoned. Roger felt tense, angry, and lonely because Margaret was so "obsessive" and could never relax and just feel close.

What Roger and Margaret didn't understand, or accept, was that they had different thresholds of intolerance for disorder, and for stress. Margaret could not relax until the house was put in order. She experienced her discomfort as a physical sensation of jitteriness and a mental preoccupation with the disorder. She would find it almost impossible to ignore the dishes the way that Roger was apparently able to do. Not only that, but she defined her need for order in terms of virtue. It was "not right" to sit down to relax until all of the household chores were completed. She "just couldn't do it."

Roger was not as disturbed by disorder. He could tolerate three days' worth of dishes piling up in the sink, and a few socks and a sweatshirt or two draped over the couch didn't really bother him. After three days, though, Roger would start to get uncomfortable with the mess, and do a whirlwind cleanup job that, although not quite up to Margaret's standards, was adequate by his standards.

Roger, for his part, has one way of managing his stress. We could call his style "hibernation." When stressed, Roger needs to go into some form of metaphorical (or actual) isolation chamber and decompress. When he's there, he experiences any interruption as a jolt of pressure, or stress. He might watch TV, or read a book, or put on the headphones. He's like a bear in a cave with a "Do Not Disturb" sign on it. A full day of work was about all he could handle without taking some down time to recharge.

Margaret, for her part, also has a way of managing stress: getting everything in order. "I just can't relax unless everything is in its place and all's right with my world." If you happen to be part of Margaret's world, she expects you to participate in this ordering, and then "we can all relax."

How does a relationship accommodate these kinds of different stress-relieving strategies? They seem to be mutually exclusive. When Margaret needs to get things in order, she expects Roger to help, *NOW!* Then they can *both* relax. When Roger needs "cave" time, he expects to be left alone until he "recharges the batteries"; then he will do whatever Margaret wants. Accommodating these kinds of conflicting needs are among the great creative challenges in any relationship.

We have a tendency, when confronted by these threshold, appetite, and style differences, to blame the other person for the behaviors that interfere with our preferred comfort strategy. Margaret called Roger's behavior, on varying occasions, "sloppiness," "laziness," "inconsiderateness," "immaturity," "selfishness," and "being just like your father." What she didn't understand was that when Roger crossed his stress threshold he experienced the discomfort as a physical buzzing in his body, an emotional feeling of irritation and aggravation and a mental sense that his brain was racing out of control with too many ideas and too much stimulation. The feeling was almost unbearable to him, and required escape. Roger labeled Margaret "compulsive," "uptight," "anal," "controlling," "tight-assed," "unable to relax," and "just like your mother." What he didn't understand was that Margaret experienced these feelings as a physical buzzing in *her* body, an aching emotional need for closure, and a set of nagging obsessive thoughts that were almost unbearable to her.

Marital Artists confronting this type of conflict of core stress management strategies might start with a conversation *during a less stressful time* (because during the stressful times the inner baby has taken control, and is driving the bus). They would make an effort to share and listen to each other and try to understand the way they each operate when stressed, what their stress relief strategies look like, and the help that each would like to get from the other. They would avoid blame or name-calling and seek understanding and acceptance of their differences. They would acknowledge that their way reflected a preference and not a universally accepted imperative. Then they would seek a mutually acceptable compromise based on an accommodation of their differences. They would make a deal and then keep it. The solution for Margaret and Roger would necessarily require a creative compromise because their two stress-relieving strategies are mutually exclusive. Perhaps Roger would push himself to not enter his cave until after he gets the house in order. Or, Margaret would push herself to be more tolerant of disorder until Roger emerged from his cave. Or, perhaps they would agree that Roger would do this on alternate evenings, and on alternate evenings Margaret would either wait for the chores to get done until Roger is ready, or she would do them herself without resentment. There may be other creative solutions involving trade-offs: paper plates, eating out, a downstairs hamper for dirty clothes; whatever. The important thing is that they shift from seeing each other as "bad" and uncooperative to seeing each other as different in their stress managing and threshold needs, and willing to cooperate. As difficult as these kinds of differences are to resolve creatively, they are certainly not helped by emotional alienation, manipulative strategies, and name-calling.

Personal Space: Affiliators and Isolators (Birds and Bears)

Among the classic conflicts that seem to arise in many marriages, especially those that present themselves in counseling, are the struggles over personal space, alone time, and being together. We are all built differently. Our comfort zones and needs for personal space are different. Since it is rare to find two individuals who share exactly the same spatial needs at the same time, we are constantly involved in a little dance that serves to maintain a spatial distance that feels comfortable to both of us. On a given occasion one partner might feel the need to be closer, while the other partner needs more space, or vice versa.

At a cocktail party, a man who was fascinated by a woman he had just met kept stepping, unconsciously and almost subliminally, in, to reduce the space between them. She, also interested, but being more conservative, kept taking a corresponding tiny step back. The distance created by her move, compelled him to eventually feel the need to step in again, and she then stepped back. An observer could watch them, gradually, over time, waltzing around the room, he stepping in, she stepping back. Eventually, the man read the body language as a sign of lack of interest. He excused himself and didn't come back. The woman, still interested and believing that they were making a good connection, was disappointed by his disappearance and over the course of the evening found a way to re-engage the man. It was clear that they were involved in a process of modulation of the dimension of personal space. When the distance felt too close, the woman pulled away; when it felt too distant, the man moved closer until he made a major move away, triggering her need to move closer.

One of the ways that these individual differences regarding personal space create conflict in relationships has to do with the management of stress. Research has demonstrated that when we are under stress, some of us seek the company of others (affiliators, "birds") and some of us want to be alone (isolators, "bears"). These seem to be profound, primitive, and unconscious impulses, and this fact has deep implications for relationships, especially when a bird is married to a bear (and they often are!).

To see how this works we need to examine a variety of situations.

Let's suppose that Mary has had a stressful day. Work stress, mother stress, kid stress, friend stress... stress, stress, stress. She comes home and her husband, Ray, is mellow as can be. He's had a great day, but he can see from the way she throws her coat down that she's fried. He says, knowing her the way he does, "Why don't you come over here and tell me what's going on." He gives her a big hug, and she starts to talk and talk about the problems of the day. She experiences a great release of pressure.

On another day the tables are reversed: Great day for Mary, awful day for Ray. She, knowing him the way she does, tells him to go out for a run and get some time for himself, and she'll handle dinner and the kids.

Clearly Mary de-stresses by connecting with Ray, and Ray de-stresses by getting away for a while. As long as one partner is in good emotional shape there is no problem. The "together one" can cover the needs of the "stressed one."

Major problems arise when both partners are stressed, depleted, and needy at the same time.

Let's look at a day when Mary and Ray are both spent. Mary comes to Ray for support; Ray moves away to seek his healing isolation. Mary moves in, seeking attention; Ray moves away, seeking respite from a demanding world. Mary, feeling rejected and abandoned (exacerbating her stress) moves in with more insistent and demanding energy. Ray, feeling harassed, overwhelmed, and smothered (exacerbating *his* stress), communicates his need for space by shutting down and putting up barriers such as newspaper, TV, nap or beer; Mary gets angry, aggressive, and accusatory. Ray gets angry, withdrawn, and accusatory. Both partners want the other to become the good mommy or daddy, who is able and willing to give them what they need. But, at the moment, both are incapable. Both have regressed into needy children. There isn't a grownup around to "fix" things. Blaming devolves into an angry sandbox fight with two inner children in a battle over who gets to be the baby, and who gets to de-stress in their preferred manner.

The lives of twentieth-century couples often involve constant stress. So the "space" problem described above is often chronic. Partners can develop stereotypical expectations about each other's tendencies to "nag," "bitch," "complain," or, conversely, to "avoid," "disappear," "shirk responsibility," "be unavailable." These perceptions create enormous resentment and angry wedges between partners who are capable of great warmth and affection during relaxed times. Many of these couples will tell me that the only time they get along well is on vacation. Vacations are the times when all of the anxiety buttons are gone, at least for a while.

Marital Artists, approaching this type of chronic problem of constitutional difference, would begin with a conversation. In the case of Mary and Ray, above, they would try to have this conversation, not in the middle of a stressed moment when they are both regressed and operating from the state of their inner child, but during a more relaxed time when they are functioning from their more transcendent, centered, adult state of being. In this way they will be able to maintain an awareness of their love for each other and their desire to find a mutually beneficial solution. In their conversation they would try to listen to each other and understand what it is like when Mary is stressed and needing closeness, and when Ray is stressed and needing space. They would avoid judgment. They would each try, creatively, to establish some kind of accommodation of the other while taking care of their own needs as well. They might develop a way of assessing whose need was greater on a given night and the other one would just "suck it up" and provide the needed environment for his or her partner; Ray might postpone his cave time for a half-hour; Mary might call a friend in order to decompress from her day; Ray might ask if he can just have a

218

half-hour of down-time and then he will give Mary his attention; they might both go out for a quiet walk together. Whatever plan they put in place would be considered a deal, and honored by both partners until a different deal is made. The most important aspects of this process, again, are that both partners communicate their love and their commitment to each other, that they refrain from blame and judgment, and understand that their partner's behavior is a reflection of constitutional differences and not of disregard or lack of concern or lack of love. This takes constant vigilance and can feel like a lot of work.

No Easy Path

The search for the easy way can be exhausting.
–Chi Shing Chen

We have been conditioned to think otherwise, but there are really no effort-free approaches to Marital Art. Life is hard. Marriage is hard. We, the most recent evolutionary models of Western men and women, simply do not want to believe this.

In order to avoid confrontation with the realistic demands of marriage, we rely on that most wonderful and ubiquitous of all psychological capabilities: *denial*. The concept of "denial" describes our ability to act as though obvious information doesn't exist, simply because it does not serve the reality we *want*. There's something wonderfully childlike about denial, like the magic in a fairy tale: "I don't like that warty reality. Be gone!"

The belief in simple, sweat-free, debt-free, guilt-free solutions almost always reflects a substantial degree of denial. "I want things to be easy, so I'll just click my heels three times and believe *real hard* in Easy." Were it only so. Unfortunately, true accomplishment in any area of life requires thoughtful preparation and hard work with a little luck thrown in for good measure. Marital Artists understand that a successful marriage is no exception.

We have become conditioned to instant gratification through the marketing of household products, electronics, drugs, credit cards, instant diets, exercise programs, and get-rich-quick schemes. We have come to accept the mythology that there are easy solutions to the difficult challenges of life.

In our marriages we must anticipate the ever-present reality of stress. We must address it in the planning of our lives, in the lifestyle choices that we make, and in the stress management opportunities that we create. Challenges and impasses will always be encountered and must be expected and embraced, transformed, or eliminated, *not* denied. In order to take the leap into marriage, it is natural, and wonderful, that the almost delusional optimism filling our hearts convinces us that we can work *anything* out. Marital Artists believes anything *can* be worked out, but that working it out requires energetic commitment to an intention and a process, and to trusting that their partner is willing to do the same.

Who you gonna believe, me or your own eyes?
—*Chico Marx*

Chapter 12: Trust and Its Vicissitudes

Trust is a fragile flower. The stem, once broken, will never be the same.
–Chi Shing Chen

In all your dealings with one another, speak the truth to one another in love, that you may grow up.
–Paul of Tarsus

Trust, in a relationship, at its most basic level, is not that much of a mystery. If both partners are trusting and trustworthy, there is unlikely to be any problem with trust in a relationship. That doesn't sound like rocket science, does it? Unfortunately, for far too many couples, trust is an issue that never gets resolved. Why is it so hard to maintain trust and trustworthiness?

Imagine if you went into a bakeshop and asked for a rye bread, you put down your money and the baker gave you a bag filled with rolled up newspapers. You probably wouldn't return to that shop. But people often spend their lives with intimate partners they don't trust. They don't trust them with sexual fidelity, with money, with the kids; they don't trust that they won't hurt their feelings, cherish their intimate communications, care about their needs, tell the truth about their comings and goings. They don't trust their loyalty. They often remain together, living parallel lives, making tentative truces in order to get through the day, but behaving, on the whole, as though they owe no allegiance to each other.

One Sunday morning George burst into the living room and said, "Dad!, Mom! I have some great news for you! I am getting married to the most beautiful girl in town. She lives a block away and her name is Susan."

After dinner, George's dad took him aside, "Son, I have to talk with you. Look at your mother, George. She and I have been married 25 years. She's a wonderful wife and mother, but, she has never offered much excitement in the bedroom, so I used to fool around with women a lot. Susan is actually your half sister, and I'm afraid you can't marry her."

George was brokenhearted. After eight months he eventually started dating girls again. A year later he came home and very proudly announced, "Diane said yes! We're getting married in June!"

Again his father insisted on another private conversation and broke the sad news. "Diane is your half sister too, George. I'm awfully sorry about this."

George was livid! He finally decided to go to his mother with the news his father had shared. "Dad has done so much harm. I guess I'm never going to get married," he complained. "Every time I fall in love, Dad tells me the girl is my half sister."

His mother chuckled, shaking her head, "don't pay any attention to what he says. He's not really your father."

The great psychologist Erik Erikson identified a series of challenges that we all must confront in the course of our psychosocial development. The first of these challenges is that of trust vs. distrust. A newly minted human essentially asks the question, "Is the world a fundamentally trustworthy place or a fundamentally untrustworthy place in which to live?" Or, in other words, "Can I trust the world to take care of me?" Erikson believed that we attempt to resolve this basic question in the context of our original caretakers, our parents or surrogate parents. If we don't resolve this issue in the direction of basic trust, then the rest of our life is likely to be a struggle. It becomes difficult to trust ourselves or others, therefore difficult to form consistent and fulfilling interpersonal relationships. So much of our relationship with another person is rooted in the ability to believe what they say and in the consistency of their motivations.

"Let's consider your age to begin with – how old are you?"

"I'm seven and a half, exactly"

You needn't say 'exactly,'" the Queen remarked; "I can believe it without that. Now I'll give you some-

thing to believe. I'm just one hundred and one, five
months, and a day."
"I can't believe that!" said Alice.
"Can't you?" the Queen said in a pitying tone. "Try
again; draw a long breath, and shut your eyes."
Alice laughed. "There's no use trying," she said; "one
can't believe impossible things."
"I dare say you haven't had much practice," said the
Queen.

–Lewis Carroll, Through the Looking Glass

Beyond the significant trust-establishing relationships of our early childhoods, we develop trust in our current relationships through experience with *this* particular person. Unconsciously, we look for congruence in the behavior of those with whom we interact. We check behavior against our experience to make sure that all elements line up. The primary cues are message content, context, and para-communications (i.e., body language, facial expression, and voice inflection). We also look for consistent outcomes. When these elements don't support each other, our radar goes up and we attempt to reconcile the inconsistencies. When we meet someone, we make hypotheses, such as, "This person seems trustworthy," or "This person looks like a crook." These hypotheses are often colored by our hopes and dreams, our fantasies and our past experiences. Our "biases" can be modified through experience (for better or worse) with any new person, but it's hard to avoid starting out with pre-conceived ideas that we learn from experience.

We develop trust in our intimate relationships subject to a few preconditions. First of all, our *ability* to trust must be intact.

Ellen had had a difficult childhood with parents who were both highly dysfunctional. Her mother had an untreated bipolar disorder, and her father was an active alcoholic. Neither parent was constitutionally capable of following through on commitments. They would frequently make promises that were just as frequently broken: to show up at a recital, to get tickets for a concert. Ellen came to expect that promises meant nothing. At the same time, her deepest wish was, like Diogenes of Greek legend, to find someone whom she could truly trust, thoroughly and completely, "an honest man."

When she met Evander she thought she had found such a man, and in truth, Evander was a good and honest man. Unfortunately, as much as Ellen wanted to believe the evidence that was reinforced for her every day, she could not relax with Evander. She kept waiting for him to disappoint her. She would often accuse him of dishonesty with very sketchy evidence (he might be 15 minutes late for a date). And, if, as happened on occasion, Evander was unable to follow through on a commitment, Ellen took it as proof of the untrustworthiness that she expected all along. Evander often felt like he just couldn't win.

Another one of the "trust" requirements is *trustworthiness*. We can get even the most trusting person to distrust us eventually if we are untrustworthy enough. Lie after lie, deceit after deceit, eventually even Pollyanna will lose her ability to trust.

In its most extreme form, chronic untrustworthiness, deceitfulness, and the manipulation of situations for personal gain, with no regard for the needs of others represents a serious psychiatric disorder called *antisocial personality disorder*. Most people who exist on the continuum of untrustworthiness are not personality disordered, they simply lack the values and self-discipline required to follow through on their commitments.

Trustworthiness is learned in early childhood, through interaction with significant caregivers and communities that value it. It used to be said that, "A man is as good as his word." Trustworthiness was discussed in terms of character and honor, qualities we don't hear very much about any more. Our society seems to value other virtues more than trustworthiness, things like accomplishment, material success, power, fame and winning. Perhaps that is why our news reports are so full of stories of lying, cheating, and manipulating in politics, finance, sports, academics, and even scientific research. Oh yes, and in love.

It is not always easy to be trustworthy. We all struggle, to greater or lesser extent, against the "demons" that cause us to act in our own immediate self-interest, against the demands of our commitments to the marital partnership. The

228

Marital Artist is in a continual struggle to behave the way s/he has promised to behave. The alternative does not support trust in a relationship: "I promised to take the dog to the vet before it closes, but I really, really want to play these last two holes of golf." "I know it's the rent money, but I have a really good feeling about this horse." "Oh, shoot! I forgot to pick up the kids." "The office will never miss this ream of paper and I'm too tired to stop at Staple's on the way home."

Both trustworthiness and trust are values held by Marital Artists, and are reflected in the choices that they make in their lives every day. Trustworthiness requires the discipline to eschew short-term benefits in order to fulfill our marital commitments and gain the rewards that come in the form of our loving trusting relationship. Trust ultimately derives from choosing a partner who is trustworthy, who maintains a sufficient level of self-control, and who is committed to keeping his or her commitments. Aspiring Marital Artists who have been burdened with a suspicious nature due to genes or past experience must develop the discipline to choose, over and over again, to trust, and give their partners the benefit of the doubt, because chronic questioning of a partner's integrity will do nothing to enhance the quality of relationships. If your partner truly is a sociopathic, cheating, lying bastard you'll know it for sure sooner or later.

It is better to conquer yourself than to win a thousand battles. Then the victory is yours. It cannot be taken from you, not by angels or by demons, heaven or hell.
—Buddha

Chapter 13: The Demons

A fish must control the movements of his tail, left and right, before he can swim in a straight line.
–Chi Shing Chen

In trying to understand the forces that keep us from trusting and behaving in a trustworthy manner, the concept of "demon" works about as well as any other. I wouldn't hold my breath until behavioral scientists or neuroscientists come up with a fool-proof explanation for, let's say, "jealousy," "rage," "vindictiveness," "selfishness," "impatience," "greed," or many of the other "demons," like addictions or mental illnesses that prevent us from behaving in our most evolved manner, and that keep us from trusting and being trustworthy. We make promises, New Year's resolutions, then lose control of ourselves over and over again, have remorse, say we're sorry.... and often really mean it. But "stuff" happens, again and again, for some of us far more often than for others.

Let's look at some of these demons. The quality that these demons share is that they all operate against our higher selves, our transcendent feelings and intentions. Behaving from our most enlightened and transcendent motives requires a great deal of insight and self-discipline. If we want to behave in loving, compassionate, generous, and respectful ways we must be aware of our feelings, and be able to stifle the impulses to act otherwise. We often expend so much energy trying to control *each other* when the real challenge lies in controlling ourselves.

Anger

In *The Dance of Anger,* Harriet Lerner says that the *feeling* of anger can alert us when essential aspects of our personal integrity are being threatened. It can impel us to make valid choices to bring balance to our lives. However, many *expressions* of anger are impulsive, infantile, manipulative, hurtful, and abusive. Such *behaviors* (not the *feelings*) can be very destructive to the integrity of relationships by violating the basic principle that "we both count." We usually use the manipulative expression of anger to serve our "smaller" selves: our greed, our impatience, our compulsiveness, our fear, our pettiness, our need to aggrandize ourselves. These impulses serve "me" at the expense of "you" or "us."

Addictions

Addictions are negative behavioral patterns over which we seem to have no control. They are very likely rooted in neurological and biochemical processes that are deep and pernicious. We are well aware of addictions to substances like drugs, alcohol, and food. We can also be addicted to the "rush" that comes from particular behaviors like gambling, sex, speeding, shopping (or shoplifting), or risk-taking. Whatever the addiction, it operates against the integrity of relationships by taking away the self-control that is at the center of deal-making behaviors. Making deals, being trust-worthy, trusting, saying what you mean and meaning what you say, making mature, sound judgments, following through, being "present" during interactions; all of these things are close to impossible for "addicts" to do consistently.

> Art told his wife, Holly, that he would definitely pick her up after her business meeting at 8:30. But Art had a serious alcohol problem and he rationalized the impulse to go into a bar at 5:30 to have, "just one," believing he'd have plenty of time to get Holly at 8:30. At 9, after one drink became many, one of his friends had to drive him home. His commitment to meet Holly was a distant memory until Holly arrived home by cab at 9:45, less than pleased. Yet again!

Trauma from the Past

We are very fragile creatures. There are so many ways that we can be hurt, physically and emotionally, and just as our bodies bear the scars of past traumas, so do our psyches and our souls. A person who has been traumatized by neglect or abuse or brutality often finds that maintaining self-control in relationships is a daunting challenge. The impulse to distrust, or to defend, or to control manipulatively emerges unbidden in many relationship contexts. For most committed couples, if the relationship is going to flourish, the task of accepting, accommodating, and adapting to past traumas in one or both partners must become a shared goal of the relationship.

Zia had been raped when she was 19. When she told Antoine about it he was very tender and understanding. He vowed to give her "all the space she needed" in coping with her trauma. But Zia's sensitivities created a constant tension in the couple's relationship and especially in their sex life. Antoine began to feel very resentful that "he just couldn't do anything right." He knew it wasn't reasonable, but he found himself very angry about "always having to walk on eggshells." He said he had thought that by being kind and considerate Zia would "get over it." He was frustrated that it wasn't working. And Zia, for her part, was constantly vacillating between rage at the rapist, anger at Antoine's lack of patience, fear of losing her relationship, and her self-critical feelings about being unable to "just get over it."

Both Zia and Antoine had to acknowledge that their expectations about Zia's "getting over it," were unrealistic. The couple's strong commitment and the

234

shared decision to enter couple's counseling, as well as Zia's entering individual therapy, and a rape survivors support group, helped the pair learn to grieve the loss of their original hopes and dreams, support Zia's recovery, and cope as a team with Zia's traumatic past.

Attachment Issues

As discussed in Chapter 8, the legacy of our earliest relationships with our parental caretakers has a profound effect on our ability to establish and maintain relationships in our later lives. When the legacy is negative, it is as though our neurological structures are formed to be compatible with the "inconsistent" or "distant" or "withdrawn" or "manipulative" relationships of childhood, but not with the more functional relationships that we hope to establish as adults. We can overcome these "wired-in" behavioral styles but, often, only with great difficulty and with the help of a professional counselor.

Psychiatric Disorders

Severe psychiatric disorders, such as schizophrenia, bipolar disorder, depression, panic disorder, obsessive-compulsive disorder, anxiety, or phobias can pose enormous challenges for a relationship. They are often tragic manifestations of complex hereditary and experiential forces and no one's fault. But they affect relationships because they diminish self-control and, consequently, deal-making and trust. Deal-making, and the trust that emanates from careful follow-through, are the essence of functionality in a relationship. Anything that impairs consistent functional deal-making and deal-keeping will damage relationships. Mental illness makes it hard to process the complex cognitive and emotional cues that comprise a relationship "deal," or allow for consistent follow-through.

In order to cope with these severe disorders, it is important for marital partners to confront them with honesty and courage. It helps to establish a support network of medical and mental health providers, family, friends and the disorder-specific support groups that exist for this purpose. Marital partners must include awareness of the disorder in the working out of their marital process. This awareness must include understanding, and a strategy for management of the cycles of symptom exacerbation and the potential for relationship disruption. This is a very difficult challenge.

Sensitivities

Sensitivities are related to the thresholds that were discussed above. The difference lies in the fact that sensitivities are not shared at all by the other partner, and may be in direct conflict, while thresholds define different levels of tolerance on a shared dimension. Often, these sensitivities seem to be out of our control, like allergies or deeply ingrained cultural conditioning. What happens if I am allergic to cats, and you have had a deep aesthetic and emotional attachment to cats since childhood? What if I can't stand disorder to the point where it makes me anxious and uncomfortable, and you're the creative type who needs to have all of your "inspirational accoutrements" around where they are handy? What if I need the peace of a rural village, and you get "juiced" by the frantic stimulation of the city?

We'd like to think that we are grown-ups, and that we can work it out. But sometimes our sensitivities have a life of their own, and are difficult to transcend by will alone. This is bad enough, and even worse when we turn our sensitivities into virtues, leading to polarization, judgment, and blame.

Steve could "not stand," to find dishes and cups on the coffee and end tables in the living room. He had to have them put away, "NOW." If nobody else would do it, then of course, he would have to do it and he resented it, displaying his displeasure with prominent, infantile displays of huffing and pouting. He had tried every means imaginable to get his wife, Trisha, to "put away her dishes when she was done." She would always say she would but she'd forget, or she'd say, "I'll do it in a few minutes," or "when the show is over." It drove Steve crazy. He believed that meticulous neatness was a universal value, and would often rage or mumble to himself and call Trisha names like "slob," or "lazy," and lecture her on how awful it was to keep such a "disaster" of a house. Trisha would respond by telling Steve to "lighten up," "get a grip," or "stop being such a con-

trol freak." Sometimes she would even be slower than usual in tidying up out of her own passive-aggressive anger. They would often withdraw from each other and remain angry for days.

Steve was a good guy and, personal demons not withstanding, aspired to a fair and equitable marriage that served both him and Trisha. Eventually, at Trisha's insistence, he agreed to attend marriage counseling. At first Steve seemed unable to take any responsibility for the problems associated with his irritability and "need for order,"and he blamed the conflict on Trisha's unwillingness to do the right thing. When he finally did identify his sensitivity as an aspect of his personality he was able to take responsibility for his behavior and say something to the effect of, "This is a sensitivity of mine. This kind of disorder in the house really makes me uncomfortable. I would appreciate it if you could be conscious of my sensitivity. I will also make a commitment to realize that you are not responsible for my sensitivity and when I see dishes in the living room, I'll have to acknowledge that I don't have a right to 'expect' you to act 'now' to alleviate my discomfort, and if I'm really uncomfortable I'll have to take care of it myself."

For her part, Trish's understanding of how uncomfortable Steve was made by disorder helped her become more compassionate and increased her moti-

vation to desist in her passive aggression. She appreciated the cessation of blame and made an effort to clean up a little more.

In these cases we have a few choices. We can enter full-out manipulative battle. We can see who can yell the loudest; who can threaten the worst consequences; see who can endure the "silent treatment" longest; we can compete to see who can call the other the most creative names... Or we can own our sensitivities and understand that there is no cosmic law stating that our partner is obligated to make everything okay.

Two Marital Artists, each taking responsibility for their own sensitivities, can probably work most things out if they remain aware that they both care about the other's well-being, comfort, and happiness, as they do their own. Their discussions, even their arguments, maintain the perspective that "they both count, all the time."

Obviously the big challenge for the Marital Artist is managing oneself... coming to terms with one's sensitivities, one's expectations of a partner; maintaining compassion for a partner's position; maintaining control of the way one communicates. These tasks can be quite challenging when the Marital Artist is "sensitive," stressed, frightened, or angry. It is then that the Marital Artist must access a mind set, a commitment to transcend reflexive and reactive behaviors. This commitment to transcend reflex and reactivity represents one of the most important values for anyone who wants to perform his or her skills at a high level. For example a young boxer must learn how not to blink when a punch is coming at his face; an opera singer must relax her vocal instrument before hitting her first note in front of a thousand people; a martial artist must relax, breathe, and dispel tension when confronted by danger; airline pilots and parents must communicate calmness and reassurance in uncertain situations where they might be expected to feel panicky. Similarly, a Marital Artist must develop the ability and self-control to communicate love, compassion, and respect even when working to address anger, hurt, or disappointment.

All of these behaviors are *counter-reflexive* and require great intention, commitment, and practice in order to achieve mastery. The ability to develop these "counter-reflexes" often distinguishes the "great" from the not-so-great, the *artists* from those of us simply struggling to go through the motions.

Entitlements

One of the complex legacies of our childhoods is our sense of entitlement. We learn from the way our parents and our culture treat us that we are, or are not, "entitled" to certain things.

Am I entitled to have doors opened for me? Am I *not* entitled to sit in the front of the bus? Can I expect that my clothes will be picked up after me or that my meals will be cooked by my partner? How about respect? Am I entitled to that? Love? Financial security? Health care?

Our sense of specific entitlements profoundly colors our choices and our behaviors in our relationships, and regardless of our higher attitudes, these unconscious expectations of entitlement can lurk behind the scenes in our relationships.

Jim was a successful businessman working on Wall Street. His brothers were also, as was their father before them. Jim's mother was a stay-at-home, caretaker mom who doted on the men of the family.

Jim was attracted to Sarah's spunk, drive, and ambition, but, in their marriage, he could not get used to her expectations. Sarah believed in a modern, equitable marriage, where both partners shared household as well as financial responsibilities. Jim also believed in this, in theory, but emotionally he felt entitled to care-taking while he provided for the family financially. He would always agree to take on his share of the household work, but when it came down to it, he would passively resist. He would find reasons not to do it, or he would postpone it, or he would forget. Because his unconscious sense of entitlement conflicted with his conscious value of a shared, egalitarian relationship, it was hard for him to acknowledge that he resented having to contribute to the maintenance work of family life.

There is a place for entitlements in our relationships: we are both entitled to the things we agree we should be entitled to. We are entitled to the fulfillment of deals. We are entitled to the love, respect, and commitment to the processes that form the foundations of our partnership. All other unspoken entitlements should be open to discussion and negotiation.

Anxiety

Anxiety represents a complex of feelings, thoughts, and sensations. In its chronic and extreme manifestations, it is a psychiatric disorder that can be disabling in its impact on our lives. Phobias are related disorders that are characterized by intense anxiety in specified contexts, such as open spaces, enclosed spaces, heights, social situations, or exposure to specific animals or objects.

Anxieties, and differing anxiety thresholds, can seriously damage relationships.

Richard had a very uncomfortable feeling of anxiety whenever he was in a social situation in which he did not know the people well. He felt uncomfortable making small talk and was constantly afraid that he would offend or commit a faux pas. He felt judged and criticized. He knew his fear was irrational, but he couldn't help it. His wife, Hillary, was very gregarious and always wanted to socialize. She could talk to anyone, and walked out of every room with a slew of new friends. Needless to say their social life was always affected by Richard's anxiety and his consequent resistance to social invitations.

Ellen is a safety freak. She fusses with the kids' clothing to protect them from the weather and she insists that the kids are never left alone even in their own yard. Her husband Tim is much more laid back. He considers himself responsible, but also believes that some risk has to be tolerated so that the kids can develop confidence and a sense of self-reliance. One afternoon they had a huge fight because Tim was more than three feet away from a small playground slide that their 4-year-old was playing on. "I can't help it," says Ellen, "a fall can happen in an instant." "Don't worry about it," says Tim, "I'm watching her." Ellen believed that Tim was being careless and irresponsible.

Anxieties can prevent us from taking actions, or tolerating situations, that we are committed to intellectually.

Elaine knew that Robert often had to work late in his retail store at the mall, but it made her very anxious whenever it happened. She worried about mishaps, accidents, and criminal assaults. She brought it up every time he had to go in late, which was sometimes three times a week. She often called her husband two or three times on these occasions, making Robert very impatient with her inability to accept and relax.

When one partner suffers from intense anxiety, the other partner is deeply affected, and often marriage counseling, or individual counseling (or even medication) is required to assist the couple in managing the anxiety as a team. The anxious partner must "own" his or her anxiety and understand that there are limits to the other partner's obligations to assuage that anxiety. That said, the Marital Artist tries to develop some level of compassion for his or her partner's anxieties, and make efforts to achieve a balance that can go a long way toward maintaining good feeling within a marriage.

Power, Control, and the Quest for Power

Most of us like to maintain a certain amount of control over our lives. We like to know where the next paycheck is coming from, as well as the next meal, and we like to know that at the end of the day there will be a roof over our heads. Beyond that there are individual differences in tolerance for disorder and chaos in our lives.

Power is a variable that is related to control. In its most positive manifestation, power provides Marital Artists with the confidence and strength to act assertively, yet lovingly and respectfully in achieving their goals and the goals of their partners. In its more negative manifestation, power contributes to the ability to manipulate and to achieve ends without concern for the well-being or rightful autonomy of the other person.

The problems begin when one person's need for power and control butts up against another person's legitimate need for autonomy in his or her own life, or against the efforts of both partners to create a shared sense of "us."

244

"Would you mind not breathing so loud?" "Stop slouching," "Don't leave your books on that table," "We're going to the mall today." There are many ways we try to control the behavior of others. Sometimes, in very dysfunctional cases, we utilize the power derived from a status advantage to get what we want.

Sid: Dale, if you don't stop buying presents for your nephew I'm going to take you off the credit card.

This kind of abuse of power in its most virulent form is manifested in actual physical or emotional abuse.

Marital Artists understand that they and their partners must, at times, be assertive, but they also respect the basic rule that "everyone counts all the time." Assertiveness means taking responsibility for your own wants and behaviors while control implies a manipulative strategy.

This is an example of control:

Kelly: Tim, you really shouldn't go to your card game tonight. You've been going out too much. If you cared at all about me you'd stay home.

In this example Kelly is controlling and manipulating Tim by appealing to some "should" injunction, and by guilt-tripping him.

This is an example of assertion:

Kelly: Tim, I'm feeling lonely and I'd like your company tonight. Would you mind canceling your card game and hanging out with me?

In this example, Kelly is taking responsibility for her want, and asking Tim, very directly, whether he will fulfill her request. Tim can say "yes" or "no" or offer another suggestion.

Advice-giving is another means of taking control. We often think that we mean well when we give other people advice. After all, we're simply "helping them" do what is best for them. There can be a control dynamic in advice giving, however, when the advice-giver assumes a status advantage, or a "one up" position while having it his or her way. In order to get around this control dynamic, the Marital Artist demonstrates love and respect for boundaries by asking permission before giving advice.

This is an example of advice-giving that is controlling:

Ron: Carol, you know, you should always put the big glasses in the back when you're loading the dishwasher.

Ron is letting his wife know that he knows how to do it and she doesn't.

This is an example of advice-giving that is not controlling:

Ron: Mind if I suggest another way of doing that?

Carol can say "go ahead", or maintain her boundary with a polite, "Thanks but no thanks. I'm fine."

This life is more than just a read through.
—Red Hot Chili Peppers

Chapter 14: Of Sex, Children, In-Laws, Vacations, and Kitchen Colors

If it is important to my beloved, then it is important to me.
–Chi Shing Chen

We can work it out.
–Paul McCartney and John Lennon

The title of this chapter barely begins to suggest the many areas of contention that partners can confront. We are *always* different people with different sensibilities, different proclivities, different wants and preferences. The Marital Artist understands this and approaches every negotiation from this perspective. He or she understands that the beloved is not wrong for wanting what he or she wants, just different.

The principles of "working it out" have been the subject of this book so far. For the Marital Artist it's all about the process of "working it out," so that when it comes to sex, kids, in-laws, vacations, and kitchen colors, it's just more of the same. Of course the stakes vary, for one or both partners, with the topic at hand, but the process doesn't.

Let's look at a few of these issues, and, with the under-standing that entire books can be (and have been) written about each one, we'll just try to get an idea about the way that the Marital Artist might approach resolving them.

Sex

Sex fills the bandwidth of our culture and our lives like few other topics, and it can cause enormous satisfaction or difficulty in our relationships. Our sexual lives emanate from the most primitive places in our beings. The longings are old and dark and complex and mysterious and worthy of deep reverence and respect. It would be nice to think that the chemical reaction that induced two individuals to start sniff-ing each other out of the pack were enough to play itself out in a symphony of sexual bliss for all of eternity. It doesn't seem to work that way for many partners. For some couples, things get in the way, things like personalities, past experi-ences, beliefs and attitudes, bio-chemistry, situational changes, bodies and their idiosyncrasies, children, emotional asynchronies, and vicissitudes of mood. Also, things change.

I would hope that lovers, planning to commit to a life to-gether, would, at the very least, *start out* with a sense of sex-ual attraction and basic compatibility; a shared compatibility of sexual preferences; a shared level of openness; an ability to communicate essential sexual wants and appetites; a de-sire and capability to please themselves and their partner. After all, for most people, the joys of physical intimacy repre-sent a core consideration in the choice to commit to another person. It helps if there is some basic level of sexual compatibility right from the start, but it is amazing what people can accomplish, sexually, with the right attitude and commitment.

We are wise to understand that what may have seemed like perfect compatibility at one phase of life can slip out of alignment during another. There are many ways that partners change, and change requires accommodation. If we can think of our sex lives as a dynamic, evolving process of shifting personal preferences and desires, we can easily see yet another passionate and exciting challenge for The Marital Artist.

Most of us require a shift to start thinking about sex as a Marital Artist does. It is uncustomary and challenging to think about our sexual proclivities as "accidents of birth," and yet most of us didn't "choose" the elements of our sexual lives. We don't choose our bodies, or our genders, or our gender preferences. We don't choose the sensitive erogenous areas of our bodies. We don't choose our sexual aesthetics. We don't choose our turn-ons and turn-offs. All of these enter and permeate our lives in mysterious ways.

We start to choose our sexual attitudes and values only as we become conscious and reflective about them. And then we can begin to shift – up to a point. It is never clear what the limits are, and in some ways it doesn't matter, because the goal is not to shatter limits for the sake of shattering limits. The goal for the Marital Artist is to create a sex life that works for both partners. Now we're back to the same principles that we have been discussing all along: everybody counts all the time; fight fair; find solutions that both partners can live with; be creative; remember that "different" doesn't equal "bad"; don't let the inner children control the dialogue; make and keep good deals; maintain love, respect, and humor even under pressure. Love. Grow.

Rick and Sonya had been married for 14 years when Sonya told Rick that she wanted to have a discussion about their sex life. Both Rick and Sonya were busy professionals and they had three children, two cars, a house, a dog, and a hamster. There were demands from community volunteer work, kids' activities, friends, and extended family. They were very busy people. They had gotten out of the habit of getting together for "dates" during which they had time to really be with and enjoy each other sexually. Their sex life generally consisted of an occasional "quickie" on Sunday mornings before the kids got up. Sonya suggested that they make a commitment to make arrangements for the kids and go on two dates a month, one of which would be a "sex date" either at home or in a motel. She said that she wanted to jazz up their sex life and lamented the loss of what used to be a very significant and exciting part of their connection. Rick thought that her plan was a great idea, and jumped on the bandwagon with a suggestion. He said that every month, on "sex night" they would bring some sexually oriented reading mate-

rial, anything they could find, from the Kama Sutra to Cosmopolitan, randomly pick an article, chapter or section, and do whatever the instructions suggested. Neither could wait for their first "date."

Because of the nature of their commitment to each other, and the trust that they had worked to develop, Sonya felt safe in bringing her issue to Rick. He was invested in the issue initially simply because he loved and respected Sonya and she brought it to him. It didn't take long before he understood that it addressed something that he, also, had been thinking about. Sonya presented her concern and shared her feelings about what she was missing without blame or criticism of either herself or Rick. Rick did not get defensive when Sonya presented her concern, but rather, listened openly, became invested in her proposal, and added a proposal of his own. They approached the issue as a team and came up with a solution that worked for both of them.

Children

Some people believe that children represent the ultimate purpose of a marriage, that marriages exist to create children. Some believe this serves the will of God, while others believe the creation of children reflects the evolutionary necessity of passing our genes on to the next generation. For many it's a deeply felt emotional "need," and for others it's an accident. Some see no need to have their own children but rather choose to support, through adoption, those who are already here. Some participate actively in the lives of the children of siblings, extended family, and friends. And some do their share by making contributions to the community of children, like coaching and teaching. Some have no interest in children at all.

For our purposes, we will discuss the problems that two partners have when trying to raise children for whom they have chosen to share responsibility. We're not going to talk about the "right" way to do it. There have been many good books written to provide parenting advice. We're going to talk about the ways that the Marital Artist approaches co-parenting, and I think that by now the approach should sound fairly familiar.

The attitudes, beliefs, sensibilities, talents, and styles that we bring to child rearing all come from someplace. They are deeply ingrained in our personalities, in who we are. The Marital Artist understands that the "I" in the "we" in that statement is always changing, learning from experience, from friends, from readings, from perceiving things in new ways. When it is acknowledged that parents are not static entities, and that children are not static entities, and that circumstances are not static, it becomes easy to see how dynamic the process of child rearing is. Parents are continually dealing with the flow of transitions and aiming at moving targets. The scale of change varies. In a day, our moods, our health, and our appetites can fluctuate. In a year clothing sizes and styles will shift. In a decade educational needs and finances can vary enormously. The Marital Artist understands that part of the co-parenting challenge is to make decisions with the partner that reflect each one's perceptions of this shifting field. This decision-making is going to require the Marital Artist's commitment to transcendent conflict resolution strategies, using all of the self-awareness and self-discipline that s/he can muster, and using the values and attitudes that characterize the Marital Artist: everybody counts all the time; fight fair; find solutions that both partners can live with; be creative; remember that "different" doesn't equal "bad"; don't let the inner children control the dialogue; make and keep good deals; maintain love, respect, and humor even under pressure. Love. Grow.

Talia and Dan's 10-year-old daughter, Michelle, had struggled in school since first grade. She seemed to have no interest in her schoolwork, although she had a great passion and talent for dance that fascinated and thrilled her parents. She had unlimited energy for her interests. She read biographies about famous dancers and she practiced all the time. She always starred in dance recitals and was developing a reputation as a serious and talented dance student. She demonstrated a quick wit, and social skills, and she had many friends, but she continued to do poorly in school even though she would profess to care that she was not getting good grades.

Talia and Dan had frequent discussions about what to do. Dan was very anxious about Michelle's poor school performance while Talia focused on what a wonderful person Michelle was, and expressed faith that she would find her way. These discussions involved a great deal of sharing by both parents about their fears, their own educational histories, their own parents' attitudes about education, their educational values, their hopes and dreams for their daughter, their attitudes about the educational system. They felt that they really understood each other's feelings, but they still did not know what to do. They decided to make an appointment for a consultation with a family therapist.

In-Laws, Vacations, Kitchen Colors, Etc.

Clearly, at this point, we could pick any of a zillion areas of potential conflict that move in and out of the lives of committed partners. Each one of them has the potential to evoke strong and passionate feelings. Each one of them has the potential to trigger old patterns of manipulative conflict resolution strategies. Each one of them can provide a potential battleground for the working out of old inner child issues. Each one of them can call back our ancient demons. Or, each one can represent an opportunity to practice Marital Art. Always keep in mind that we are works in progress. We will often fail in our efforts to maintain the highest ideals of the Marital Art. This is to be understood with a spirit of humor, compassion, forgiveness, and renewed commitment to begin the process yet again.

Love of beauty is taste. The creation of beauty is art.
—*Ralph Waldo Emerson*

Chapter 15 - The Long View: Staying Together

When a sinuous vine wraps itself around a sturdy tree, over time the two become as one. They can not be separated without damaging the tree or the vine or both.
–Chi Shing Chen

Love seems the swiftest, but it is the slowest of all growths. No man or woman really knows what perfect love is until they have been married a quarter of a century.
–Mark Twain

Many older cultures have resolved the problem of sustaining the marital commitment by stabilizing the institution of marriage, as opposed to focusing on the happiness of the individuals. Severe and rigid divorce and adultery laws (some even involving hideous mutilations or death sentences for transgressors), arranged marriages, rituals of seeking parental approval, dowries, sacred community marriage ceremonies all contribute to a context of "seriousness" of commitment and presuppose community involvement and support. Further, in these marriages, members of the community share expectations that foster stability, at least in terms of continuity of the marriage, if not continuity of emotional closeness.

Western marriages in our time are often unsupported in these powerful ways. And even if we go through the motions, as in $50,000 weddings, the structural bonds that hold our marriages together are often superficial and weak.

We can reduce the odds of divorce if we plan ahead and if we have some good luck before the wedding: Marry a little older, rather than very young; have at least a reasonable amount of money so that you are not scrounging all the time just to survive; come from loving and supportive families; take a pre-marital course. There are other factors that will contribute to keeping a marriage together. But Marital Artists are not at all interested in simply staying together for the sake of staying together. They are deeply invested in the quality of their committed life together. I would suspect that most of us, given the choice, would prefer that our relationship be a wonderful one. Why would anyone choose to remain in a long life together that is somewhere between "Eh, okay" and horrible?

Getting Your Partner to Change

The relentless pounding of the sea will never transform the shoreline into a mountain. It will simply grind it down and push it away.
–Chi Shing Chen

*Occasionally, I allowed myself to think of the prom-
ise I had made to myself at the altar-- to create a
husband who would be totally compatible.*
–Erma Bomback

Marital artists do not expend a great deal of energy in trying to change their partners. They may hope things will change. They may request change and work hard to articulate their feelings about why they would like change and what it would mean to them. It is then up to the partner to make the choice to change. Among those lucky partners who skate through life gracefully and happily, there is usually a shared commitment to a process of change that will benefit both.

It is easy to attribute our marital problems to the awful things our partner is doing wrong. If only he or she would shape up! This may even be true, although, as previously stated, *we can never compel our partner to change,* although he or she always has the power to work on changing him- or herself. If s/he demonstrates egregious behaviors destructive to him- or herself, to you or to the relationship, and s/he refuses to work on change in response to your requests and shared feelings, it might say something about his or her commitment to the relationship and some counseling may be in order, preferably for the couple, but, if not, for whichever partner is willing to go. If your partner is just being him- or herself, with habits that are not particularly destructive (though perhaps annoying to you) and you can't work on *yourself* enough to accept who s/he is, then maybe the problem is more about you, and again, counseling may be helpful. Developing grace in the performance of this dance is close to the center of the Marital Art.

Every day Eve would go out to the lemon tree that she had planted in her back yard years before. She desperately wanted to eat a sweet, firm apple, and every day all she found were lemons. She was always disappointed and became furious. She would scream at the lemon tree and tear at its branches and throw rocks at it and still there was nothing but lemons. She would rage and cry and then go home and tell all her friends what an awful tree it was; that she could not get a single apple from the tree no matter what she did. And, she would tell her friends over and over again, how much she did for that tree. Yes she did. She watered it, and picked the weeds, pruned it, and sprayed it with organic sprays to keep the bugs away. Why wouldn't it give her apples? Her friends would remind her as kindly as they could that she had planted a lemon tree. Eve would just shake her head. Next day she would go out again and hope for apples.

Most people have a hard time comprehending that the person that they chose is really, in all probability, notwithstanding a radical act of God or Nature, the person they are going to have to live with in this relationship. The person may change (for the better or worse), but *you* will have nothing to do with that change, unless your partner chooses to let you. Not infrequently I hear in counseling that a spouse is unbearable to live with.

"He's unbearable," says she.
"Oh, yes? Why," ask I.
"He's such an irresponsible child."
"Is that any different from the way he was when you met him?" I ask.
"Not really," she says.
"So why do you think you were attracted to him?"
"My family was so stuffy and compulsive. He was a riot. I was crazy about him."
"Oh," say I.

I have found, over and over again, that the very qualities that attract us in the first place are inevitably the ones that drive us crazy someplace down the road. A man who is attracted to the sexy, flirtatious siren, spends his life outraged because she can't seem to help attracting and flirting with other men; or, the woman who loves her man's work ethic and material success becomes outraged that he seems to be a workaholic who has no time for her or the family; the clown who was so amusing in the beginning won't take anything seriously and seems silly, insubstantial, and irresponsible; the dreamy, romantic poet who once made her starry-eyed, accomplishes nothing and seems depressed; the organized, competent, get-things-done gal who helped him get his life together, starts to seem compulsive, rigid, and controlling. Doesn't it seem like we just can't win?

It is because of our own ambivalences that we put so much energy into trying to change our partners. If we could only get the successful guy to be a little more caring and attentive at home; if we could get the sexy gal to tone it down in public; and so on...

Just like Eve in her quest for apples, we persist, day after day, year after year, in going out into the backyard looking disdainfully at the old lemon tree. Every time we find lemons we're disappointed. Imagine that: lemons again. Guess I'll try tomorrow. Pretty foolish, you say? Any more foolish than expecting that your irresponsible, fun-loving partner is suddenly going to become a paragon of commitment, dedication, and responsibility? Maybe he'll change if you yell loud enough, or pout, or point out how responsible your sister's husband is. Or maybe your wife will stop flirting if you call her a "whore" or threaten to cheat on her with her best friend, "who thinks I'm pretty darn cute, by-the-way-in-case-you-haven't-noticed!" Maybe they'll change. Or maybe they won't, and you'll have spent a lot of time yelling, or pouting, or threatening, or calling names and creating a pretty toxic environment down on the homestead.

And here's an even scarier thing to consider: As hard as it is to get your partner to change, it may feel like it's worth the energy, because it seems like a better bet than getting yourself to change. It might be easier to pressure and nag your husband to be more responsible than it would be to get yourself to care less about it, to embrace the chaos of your life or to shrug your shoulders and love him for his good qualities; it's easier to call your wife "whore," than to come to terms with your own need to control, and to conquer your sexual insecurities and fears of abandonment.

Or, if your partner really does turn out to be a true lemon, then it might be less frightening to "bitch and moan" than it would be to dump him/her.

Marital Artists can certainly request change from their partners. They can share their thoughts and feelings about the behaviors at issue. But if our partners demur, most of us have a hard time accepting that they are not ready or willing, and that we need to let it go. The alternative is to move on to the next level and employ strategies of manipulation. We threaten, we yell, we nag, we demand, we pout, we withhold love. The problem with manipulation is that it doesn't work. Well, it may work in the short run, but in the long run it creates a scummy residue of hostility, resentment, and contempt, which are death to relationships. If your partner doesn't take on the task of changing because s/he wants to, after understanding how his or her behavior bothers or hurts you, or if you can't learn to accept him/her as she is, then you have a limited set of options: You can bring your issues to counseling, you can get out of the relationship, or you can play out the war in animated misery until one of you dies (which will happen eventually) or sees the error of his/her ways in a flash of insight delivered by God during one of those 40-day-and-night walks through the desert. Change can also happen when your partner talks to a good friend or a therapist, or meditates on a sunset, or observes the bad (or good) behavior of other couples, or reads a book, or gets older and tireder and/or wiser. But *you* won't change them.

Another option is to choose the right person in the first place. This is not an easy solution (especially after twelve years of marriage), but it does make some sense. You need to know yourself ("I like apples more than I like lemons"), and you need to know your partner ("He's the apple of my eye!"). More specifically, you need to know more than the scrubbed character that shows up on your first five dates.

> *A young woman came to Vermont in August, on her summer vacation. She swam in the lakes and walked the mountain trails. She smiled at the birds and bathed in the fragrance of wildflowers. She sat and dreamed under sunny blue skies.*
>
> *"This is a wonderful place," she whispered to herself. "I've always wanted to live in a place just like this."*
>
> *She went back to her home, packed everything, and moved her life to Vermont.*
>
> *It was like Heaven.*
>
> *She said, "Nothing can be better than this. I've never been so happy."*
>
> *As she basked in the waning beauty of the Vermont summer, she thought, "I will never need anything else."*
>
> *And then, with the approach of autumn, the leaves began to change color. The young woman was*

thrilled and amazed by the transformation. It was as though she was adrift in a sea of beauty and it intoxicated her. The summer was all she needed, but this... it surpassed her wildest imaginings. She could not believe the good fortune that brought her to Vermont. "Oh, how I love my life," she exclaimed.

But, day-by-day the north wind blew colder and the colorful leaves, which had already dulled to a mono-chromatic brown, began to fall to the ground. Now the slate gray skies began to powder the earth with snow. At first, this winter landscape, too, seemed beautiful. The young woman, though apprehensive, decided that she could learn to take nourishment from the icy charm of this cold, white season. But, as the snows continued to accumulate, and the drifts grew, and the winds howled, she felt a weary isola-tion and loneliness. She was fatigued by the effort required to live in this demanding environment. "I'm so weary. Maybe moving to Vermont was not such a smart idea," she sighed.

Just as she was about to sink into the darkest corner of her despair, she smelled the first clean breeze of spring. "Thank goodness," she said, "I didn't think I could take much more." Sure enough the snow melted, and then it melted some more. Before she knew it, the young woman was up to her axles in mud. There was mud on her shoes and mud on her floors, dust in her hair, in her bed and in her crunchy granola. The slurping, burping mud just made her shake her head. "How could I have been such a fool?" she asked no one in particular.

But mud eventually gives way to crocuses and daffodils. The young woman blinked through her mud-streaked window at the promise of a new beginning. The spring exploded into blossom and she found herself smiling again, almost all the time. Finally the summer returned and the young woman's excitement could not be contained. "Maybe now I'll remember why I moved here," she said. But, the year before, she had arrived in Vermont after the black flies had come and gone. When the little skin-gobbling specks buzzed their enthusiasm at meeting her, she was not amused. In fact, she was beside herself with frustration and rage. She pulled her hair, smashed her dishes, and stomped on the ground. Then she packed her bags. "Maybe the cold," she said; "Maybe the mud. But I can never learn to accept the black flies. Never! Never! Never!"

When she arrived home she unpacked and breathed a sigh of relief. "Vermont seemed so perfect when I saw it in August. Oh, well."

Soon after the young woman settled back in to her old familiar place, she met a young man. He was thoughtful and considerate and generous and gentle and strong and handsome and talented and wealthy.

"This is a wonderful man," she whispered to herself. "I've always wanted to live with a man just like him."

If only our partners could remain the way they were when we fell in love. Oh, it would be so lovely. They would open doors, and buy us flowers, cook for us and smile lovingly; talk endearingly, touch us tenderly. They would never get angry or frustrated. They would never think of themselves. Just us. It often takes a while before we see most of the seasons of a person, even though the seasons are inevitable. How does your partner behave when s/he is frustrated, angry, disappointed, stressed, humiliated, shamed, needy, aroused, grumpy, hormonal, competitive? How does he or she behave in different contexts: with his or her family of origin, at work, in restaurants, with *your* family, with subordinates and authorities, in the company of old friends?

The Marital Artist must understand and accept all of a partner's seasons, or at least be familiar enough with them to know that s/he can live with them.

Fear

Clearly, Marital Art presupposes an environment of safety. Fear on the part of one or both partners represents the essence of dysfunction in a marriage.

Fear can be a response to threats of physical abuse, threats of financial consequences, threats related to the well-being or custody of children, threats of embarrassment, threats of harm to a reputation, threats of shaming, threats regarding property, threats involving withholding of love or support, threats of demeaning criticism and derisive judgment, threats of suicide, and threats of physical symptoms or self-abuse through negative or dangerous habits.

An atmosphere of fear destroys any hope of achieving even a moderately functional partnership. If you are seeking a marriage that aspires to Marital Art, and you are caught in a cycle of abuse and fear, or if you are unable to leave a bad marriage because you are afraid, you should seek professional help immediately.

Loneliness and Its "Solutions"

In addition to the above-mentioned fears, we must spend a moment discussing the fear of loneliness. Many people enter marriages with unsuitable partners in the first place simply to avoid loneliness. Or, they try to tolerate the deep and agonizing loneliness that results when they find themselves stuck in emotionally unfulfilling marriages, unable to make changes or unwilling to leave. The inability to tolerate loneliness motivates some of our worst choices. For instance, sometimes, in an effort to assuage the pain of loneliness, we develop soul-numbing habits or addictions, or we become embroiled in a dramatic quest for new love.

In an effort to compensate for marital patterns of emotional distance, isolation, and poor communication, some people try to fill themselves up with potentially addictive pastimes in order to anesthetize their loneliness. These might include alcohol, food, drugs, sex, compulsive shopping, exercise, internet, and gambling. This is not the place to discuss the consequences of relying on any of these habits to assuage loneliness, but suffice it to say, there is a downside to all of them.

Time Together

For you, my love, I will sculpt time out of stone.
–Chi Shing Chen

Marital Artists understand that there is no art, and hardly any marriage, unless partners make the effort to spend time together. It is very easy to get caught up in the world of busyness with demanding work schedules, children, homes, cars, pets, friends, exercise, shopping, cleaning, maintaining... exhausting lives. And with all of these demands on time it is easy to put our marriages on the shelf like the ceramic vase we got for a wedding gift. The marriage feels like something we have and it's easy to take for granted. We maintain our expectations, however, that our partners will be there when we need them to pick up the kids, clean the dishes, or rub our aching back. Then we're surprised and disappointed, on those rare occasions that we do have time for our partners, that they feel emotionally distant and unavailable.

If we neglect to set aside time for each other, we lose touch and feel like we are low priority in each other's busy lives. We do not have the opportunity to share and keep abreast of the changing textures of each other's lives and we

271

don't get the opportunity to say and do the things that let each other know where we stand, that we care about each other, that we are partners, friends, lovers.

When partners first met, it used to be exciting to look forward to "dates," or opportunities to "hang out." In a long-term relationship, making, and then preparing for dates (hang-out time) can build positive anticipation and keep the romantic fires smoldering. Dates can even set up the possibility that hot, passionate flames can be ignited. Of course time together is not always positive and affirming, unless both partners choose to make it that way. These "dates" must be approached with an intention to stay away from provocative hot-button issues, and efforts must be made to create an emotional environment that feels good for both partners. Contentious "issues" can be dealt with another time.

Staying together over time can have the quality of an ongoing heated war, of a cool, distant business relationship, or any number of other arrangements. Marital Artists prefer to make and share the time with each other that will maintain closeness and permit their transcendent process to unfold.

Sustaining Marital Art

Happy marital partners repeatedly cite certain factors in explaining their relationship success. These include the idea that they like their partner as a friend, that they believe in their commitment to each other and take it seriously, that they continue to build emotional and sexual intimacy over time, that they laugh together, that they affirm one another and share the problems of finances, household chores, children, in-laws, and other life challenges. These factors seem very close to the practices of the Marital Artists we have been discussing throughout this book.

Friendship and Commitment

Partners who have chosen to stay with each other after the biochemical love-rush has cleared, may find that they like and respect each other for the people that they are; that they work and play well together, and care deeply about each other's well being. They may discover that they share goals and values, especially the ones that support and enhance their marriage. They may find that they are both committed to helping each other have a great life, and to grow individually and as a couple. They are tolerant and compassionate about each other's shortcomings, or as one friend put it, "She accepts my bullshit and I accept hers." They each acknowledge the accidents of their birth and work together to transcend them. They discover that the roaring fire of early romantic passion can continue to smolder and periodically burst into flames, and they come to appreciate the dance of sexual appetite and desire that inevitably shifts forward and back and is stimulated by an appreciation of differences. They may find that they accept the differences that are intrinsic in their individual make-ups, and although these differences may occasionally lead to conflict, they are committed to fighting fairly and seeking mutually acceptable resolutions. They understand the paradox that winning can be losing and losing can be winning. They employ thoughtful, respectful, non-manipulative conflict resolution strategies. They recognize that they both count, *all the time,* and they maintain an awareness that they are *always* married and responsible to the welfare of the marriage, *all the time.* They understand that stresses are inevitable, and that stressors for one become stressors for both. They expect and embrace change in every aspect of their lives. They work to become a more and more creative problem solving team. These are the Marital Artists.

Throughout the world sounds one long cry from the heart of the artist: Give me the chance to do my best.

—From Gabriel Axel's film, Babette's Feast

Chapter 16 – The Marital Artist

An artist has got to be careful to never really arrive at a place where he thinks he's at somewhere. You have to realize that you're always in a state of becoming.
–Bob Dylan speaking in Martin Scorcese's film, *No Direction Home*

Marital Artists are visionaries and creators of lives. They seek to develop their hearts, minds, bodies, and souls so as to employ themselves in a project larger than themselves. It is not an immersion in the couple, it is not a loss of self, it is a joining, a sharing, the acceptance of a challenge to create a couple, a partnership that is greater than either individual. Within the context of relationship, and using the creative outlook of the artist, the partners seek to learn about themselves and each other, to digest all that came before in order to transcend and construct something larger.

Marriage is more like a dance that never ends than a painting that gets completed, framed, and hung on a wall. It starts with an intention and is recognized as a perpetual work in progress. The goal is not to have your marriage hung in a museum, but to exult, together, in the joy of creation and continual re-creation. The Marital Artist revels in the processes of loving.

The Way of the Marital Artist

Marital Artists have made a life decision involving a quality of commitment to their relationship that is all-encompassing. This is a personal decision in the same realm as the decision to live a healthy lifestyle, work for social change, or join a religious group. The decision reflects a set of deep values, which imply subsets of obligations and responsibilities.

Marital Artists commit to the discipline of their art because they have faith in the benefits that this path will provide for them in their lives and in the lives of their children and others whom they touch. The lifestyle represents a practice, an ideal, a vision of potential that we work toward on a daily basis. It is difficult and challenging and fun, and the payoffs, both for the individual Marital Artists and their relationships, can be transformative and transcendent.

Marriage is hard enough, and we need a core commitment that is bigger than ourselves to get us through the hard times. When, together, we find ourselves at those impasses that make us want to scream, "Why bother?" It helps to be able to appeal to a shared sense of purpose, a bigger purpose, a purpose that transcends the petty wants and "needs" of the moment. A commitment to the shared journey of transcendence can supply that purpose, a commitment to move beyond our perceived wants and needs and strive for a larger

278

view of our lives. Those with a deep religious or spiritual heritage may already understand the nature of this transcendent purpose. They understand, in terms that fit their worldview, that it is possible to adopt, or construct, an ideal self and a path that leads them beyond reflexive and unexamined choices.

For those without a religious foundation the meaning must be constructed. An example of such a meaning can be simply stated as follows:

We are making this commitment so that we may have partnership and company on our journeys, help each other become the best people we can be, and have the best lives that we can have.

In this chapter I would like to outline some of the ways that Marital Artists can practice their art. There are many areas of daily life that provide opportunities, and since the work is primarily inner work, much of it can be done alone as well as with the partner.

Marital Artists know that they have a choice.

Marital Artists have *chosen* to pursue the Marital Arts. It is not required and won't be on the test. They understand that the commitment implied by this choice is not an easy one and requires consciousness and intention. They understand that they are walking through a doorway, entering a mental space, and making a spiritual commitment that will color all their future decisions. Marital Artists have accepted the new goals, with their partners, of developing the self-discipline to transcend the accidents of birth, and of pursuing a larger life.

Marital Artists are committed to the discipline.

Change is challenging and Marital Artists are committed to adapting to change. Developing the ability to resist reflexive or unexamined action and make choices that serve the Art, takes discipline. Our natural tendency is to do things the way we have always done them, or the reflexive ways that come most naturally. Like a wheel in a rut, our direction is most easily determined by forces outside ourselves. Marital Artists aspire to take control of the wheel and determine its direction while understanding that the wheel will tend to return to the rut. The process of staying out of the rut requires daily intention and the exercise of self-discipline.

Marital Artists understand the nature of trust and the fundamental importance of deals.

Marital Artists know that trust is the foundation of relationship, and mistrust can pollute all aspects of the partnership. They understand that the deals made by partners are the tangible manifestations of trust, and they don't take deals lightly. This respect for deals starts with the marital vows. When Marital Artists think about their promise to love, honor, and respect their partners, they understand that that means following through when they are tired or cranky or sick or angry as well as when they feel close, loving, and in sync. This commitment to honor deals takes enormous self-discipline and requires daily practice.

Marital Artists understand that, "We all count, all the time."

Our inner children want what they want when they want it. They will often resort to any kind of manipulative strategy to achieve the goal, without concern for the needs of the other. They will even "throw their partner to the bear" in order to get out of a bad spot. Marital Artists understand that allowing their inner children to control the interaction usually leads to poor outcomes, erosion of trust, and lingering resentment. Marital Artists aspire to acknowledge, respect the wants of their partners, and negotiate from their highest selves, even when they are weakened by stress or fatigue or frustration.

Marital Artists are committed to self-awareness.

It is difficult to share yourself with another person unless you know yourself. Marital Artists are committed to developing a third eye, to monitor their feelings, thoughts, sensations, memories, hopes, fears, ambivalences, fantasies, wants, and dislikes, which perpetually flow through them. Maintaining awareness helps keep communications accurate, faceted, subtle, and complete. Awareness permits the Marital Artist to avoid the reactive and reflexive interactions that create negativity, defensiveness, resentment, and emotional distance.

Marital Artists take responsibility for their actions, words, feelings, decisions, and intentions.

It is tempting and often easy to avoid responsibility. "The devil made me do it." "Well if you hadn't looked at her that way, I never would have set your car on fire." "If you hadn't hidden the checkbook, I would have paid the mortgage."

Victimization does happen; it's what we do in the face of that victimization that defines our character. Marital Artists understand that they move closer to their transcendent selves when they own their behavior, and come as close as possible to true transparency in their interactions with their partners. The partner's response cannot be controlled, but can be folded in to the next round of communication.

Marital Artists know how to let go and move on.

Marital Artists understand the precariousness of all human endeavors. No matter how committed we may be to creating Marital Art, and no matter how much energy we put into taking responsibility for our actions, we will often fail. Therefore Marital Artists work to develop the capacity to accept, apologize sincerely, forgive, let go, and move on, while trusting that we are all doing the best we can. If someone truly cannot trust that their partner is trying his/her best then they must understand that the relationship has to move through *this* impasse, perhaps with the help of counseling, before Marital Artistry can be achieved.

Marital Artists understand that a marriage is a process rather than a "thing."

A relationship is not a static entity. It moves and flows, sometimes hot sometimes cold, sometimes it works, sometimes not so well. Marital Artists understand that awareness of and commitment to the process help maintain the relationship through its various states. As breakdowns, and impasses are inevitable, Marital Artists grow to expect them. Marital Artist are able to stop the car, get out, clear the road, or get under the hood and make repairs. There is no dirty fighting, no old laundry bags of unresolved issues, no holding on to hurt feelings, no damage to trust. Just an understanding that two imperfect people who love each other and are committed to working through the impasses can do so and emerge from the other side with their love and respect intact, and even enhanced.

Marital Artists understand the randomness of the accidents of birth.

None of us choose our beginnings. We do not choose our parents, our time in history, our race, national origin, gender, size, hair color, our physical or intellectual endowments, the religion we are born into, our language, the books and TV we are exposed to when very young.... The list goes on. Marital Artists feel grateful for the gifts they have received and philosophical about their deficiencies, "accepting those they can not change, and working to change the ones they can." They feel especially grateful for having been inspired to grow beyond these accidents and they make the choice to do so over and over again. They understand that there is often a great impetus to identify with these accidents, even a pride or humiliation in this identification, which can take control over their lives. Marital Artist do not judge these accidents in themselves or in others. They accept that these accidents of birth are simply starting points. Marital Artists view marriage as an opportunity for each partner to develop the shared transcendent qualities of humor, creativity, compassion, acceptance, forgiveness, generosity, empathy, and, of course, love.

May your marriage be transformed into glorious art. Good luck.

Here's to matrimony, the high sea for which no compass has yet been invented!
—*Heinrich Heine*

The Marital Artist's Creed

I have chosen to be a Marital Artist.

I intend to develop myself within my loving partnership, and strive for the highest levels of awareness, compassion and loving action.

I aspire to know myself so that I can transcend the accidents of my birth, and strengthen my self-discipline in order to achieve the fullest actualization of myself and my partner.

I will try never to forget that the time we have together is short.

I will practice empathic being, patient understanding and loving action so that both my partner and I may grow and flourish together.

I will strive for presence and artistry in the significant and insignificant details of my committed loving relationship.

In times of stress, anger and disagreement, as well as in times of joy and connectedness, I will maintain awareness that we both count all the time.

When there is contention, I will fight lovingly, fairly, and respectfully and strive for outcomes that serve us both.

Although I love and cherish my inner child and will invite him on all of my journeys, I will not let him/her drive the van.

Every day I will challenge myself to be creative in order to fill our lives with joy and love.

Art Enables us to find ourselves and lose ourselves at the same time.
—*Thomas Merton*

Bibliography

Atkinson, Brent, Altered States, *Psychotherapy Networker, Sept./Oct. 2004*

Ausubel, Nathan, A Treasury of Jewish Folklore, *1948 New York, Crown Publishers, Inc.*

Berne, Eric, Games People Play: The Psychology of Human Relationships, *1964, Grove Press, New York*

Berne, Eric, Transactional Analysis in Psychotherapy, *1961 Grove Press, New York*

Bombeck, Erma, A Marriage Made in Heaven, or Too Tired for an Affair, *New York, Harper Collins Publishers, Inc. 1993*

Bradshaw, John, Homecoming: Reclaiming and Championing Your Inner Child, *1990, Bantam Books, New York*

Bronson, Po, Merryman, Ashley, Will This Marriage Last? *Time in Partnership with CNN, http://content.time.com/time/nation/article/0,8599,120978 4,00.htm*

Buber, Martin, I and Thou, *New York, Charles Scribner and Sons, 1970*

Carroll, Lewis, Alice in Wonderland and Through the Looking Glass, *Kingsport, TN, Grosset and Dunlap, Inc. 1946*

Chabad-Lubavitch, *Why Marry? The Call From Within, http://www.chabad.org/library/article_cdo/aid/448425/j ewish/Why-Marry.htm*

Chapman, Gary, The 5 Love Languages: The Secret to Love that Lasts, *Northfield Publishing, Chicago, IL, 2010*

Cherlin, A.J., Chase-Lansdale, P.L., & McRae, C (1998). Effects of parental divorce on mental health throughout the life course. *American Sociological Review, 63, 239-249.*

Coontz, Stephanie, Marriage, A History, *New York, Viking, 2005*

Erikson, Erik, Childhood and Society, *New York, W.W. Norton and Co. Inc, 1950*

Fisher, Helen, Why We Love, *New York, Holt, 2004*

Ford, Richard, The Sportswriter *New York, Vintage, 1986*

Frankl, Viktor E., Man's Search for Meaning, *New York, Washington Square Press, Inc., 1967*

Friel, John C.; and Friel, Linda D., The Seven Best Things (Happy) Couples Do, *Deerfield Beach, FL, Health Communications, Inc., 2002*

Fuller, R. Buckminster, The Operating Manual for Spaceship Earth, *1963*

Gottman, John, Why Marriages Succeed or Fail, *New York, Simon and Schuster, Inc. 1995*

Gottman, John The Seven Principles for Making Marriage Work, *New York, Crown Publishers, 1999*

Gray, John, Men Are From Mars, Women Are From Venus, *New York, Harper Collins, 1992*

Harley, Willard F. Jr. His Needs, Her Needs: Building an Affair Proof Marriage, *Old Tappan, New Jersey, Flemming H. Revell Co. 1986*

Harris, Gardiner Out-of-Wedlock Birthrates Are Soaring, U.S. Reports, *New York Times, May 13, 2009*

Heaton, T. B. (1990). Marital stability throughout the child-bearing years. *Demography, 27, 55-63*

Kuerer Gangi, Barbara, Intimate and Marital Attachment: Application of Infant Attachment Research Findings to Understanding the Development and Dynamics of Adult Love Relationships, *Ph.D. Thesis, Cincinnati, OH, Union Institute and University, 2002*

Lerner, Harriet G., The Dance of Anger, *New York, Harper Collins Publishers, Inc., 1985*

Maslow, Abraham H. Toward a Psychology of Being, *New York, J. Wiley And Sons, 1999*

McLanehan, S., & Sandefur, G. *(1994)*, Growing up with a single parent: What hurts, what helps. *Cambridge, MA: Harvard University Press.*

Mehrabian, Albert, Nonverbal Communication. *Chicago: Aldine-Atherton. 1972*

Miles, Linda,; Robert Miles, Robert, The New Marriage : Transcending the Happily-Ever-After Myth, *Fort Bragg,Cypress House, 2000*

Miller, Michael Vincent, Intimate Terrorism. *New York: W. W. Norton, 1995*

The Stanford Encyclopedia of Philosophy, *http://plato.stanford.edu/entries/love/*

Strauch, Barbara, The Primal Teen: What the New Discoveries About the Teenage Brain Tell Us About Our Kids, *New York, Doubleday, 2003*

Taylor, Maurice and McGee, Seana, The New Couple, *New York, Harper Collins, 2000*

Tjaden, P., & Thoennes, N. (2000). Full report of the prevalence, incidence, and consequences of violence against women, *Washington, DC: National Institute of Justice and Centers for Disease Control and Prevention.*

US Census Bureau, 2010, Statistical Abstract: Births, Deaths, Marriages, & Divorces, http://www.census.gov/compendia/statab/cats/births_de aths_marriages_divorces.html

Viorst, Judith, Grown Up Marriage. *New York: The Free Press, 2003*

Waite, L. J., Browning, D., Doherty, W. J., Gallagher, M., Luo, Y., & Stanley, S. M. (2002). Does divorce make people happy? Findings from a study of unhappy marriages. *New York, NY: Institute for Aerican Values.*

Waite, Linda J. and Gallagher, Maggie, The Case for Marriage, *New York, NY, Doubleday, 2000*

Waite, L. J., & Lillard, L.A. (1991). Children and marital disruption. *American Journal of Sociology, 96, 930-953.*

Walsh, David,; Bennett, Nat, WHY Do They Act That Way? : *A Survival Guide to the Adolescent Brain for You and Your Teen, New York, Free Press, 2004*

Watzlawick, Paul,; Beavin Bavelas, Janet,; Jackson, Don J.; Pragmatics of Human Communication, *New York, Norton, W. W. & Company, Inc., 1967*

Winerman, Lea, The Minds' Mirror, *Monitor on Psychology, Vol. 36 #9, pp 48-50, October 2005*

CPSIA information can be obtained at www.ICGtesting.com
Printed in the USA
LVOW10s1615030516

486489LV00021BA/712/P